Acknowledgements

The publishers gratefully acknowledge permission from the following sources for publishing copyright material:
A & C Black for 'Whirling leaves' from *Acting Rhymes*, 'Miss Polly' and 'Can you tell me' from *Okki Tokki Unga*, and 'She fell into the bath-tub' from *Nonsense Rhymes*; The Bodley Head for 'Lollipop lady' from *I Din Do Nuttin*; Bogle-L'Ouverture Publications for 'Milk' and 'Humming-bird' from *Rain Falling, Sun Shining*; Hamish Hamilton for 'The triangle song' from *Playalong Songs*; Hamlyn Publishers for 'Thunder' from *Rhyme Time*; The Islam Centre for 'Hind Desh' from *Hinduism*; Macdonald & Co for 'Teddy Bear' from *Leon Baxter's Book of Nonsense*; Paxton House for 'Slowly, slowly' from *Playway to Rhythmics*; Penguin Books for 'Two little boats', 'One morning', 'Here is a steamroller', 'A tiny, tiny worm', and 'Help me wind my ball of wool, from *This Little Puffin . . .*; Brenda I. Piper for 'Stamping' from *Sing as You Grow* (Ward Lock Educational); Tindal Press for 'Stirring' from *Rhythm Rhymes*.

Every effort has been made to trace and acknowledge contributions. If any right has been omitted, the publishers offer their apologies and will rectify this in subsequent editions following notification.

Starting with Rhyme

Linda Mort & Janet Morris

Bright Ideas
FOR Early Years

Published by Scholastic Publications Ltd,
Villiers House, Clarendon Avenue,
Leamington Spa, Warwickshire
CV32 5PR

© 1991 Scholastic Publications Ltd

Written by Linda Mort and Janet Morris
Edited by Janet Fisher
Sub-edited by Kim Daniel
Designed by Sue Limb
Illustrations by Jane Bottomley
Photographs by Richard Butchins

Cover photography by Martyn Chillmaid
Printed by Loxley Brothers, Sheffield

British Library Cataloguing in Publication Data
Mort, Linda
 Bright ideas for early years: starting with rhyme.
 1. Primary schools. Activities
 I Title   II Morris, Janet
 372.1332

ISBN 0-590-76435-7

Contents

Introduction

Music, songs and rhyme have always held a unique place in young children's learning. From the first gentle bounces on an adult's knee to the words of 'Round and round the garden', a baby is involved in active communication with another person in a very enjoyable way. Throughout the early years, the enormous variety of nursery rhymes and songs offers children ways to develop their social skills, as they learn to take turns and interact with one another. On the emotional level, too, rhymes and songs which are special to a child, perhaps because they become part of bedtime routines, can be a source of reassurance and comfort. Some poems and songs, like stories, can help children to overcome worries and fears.

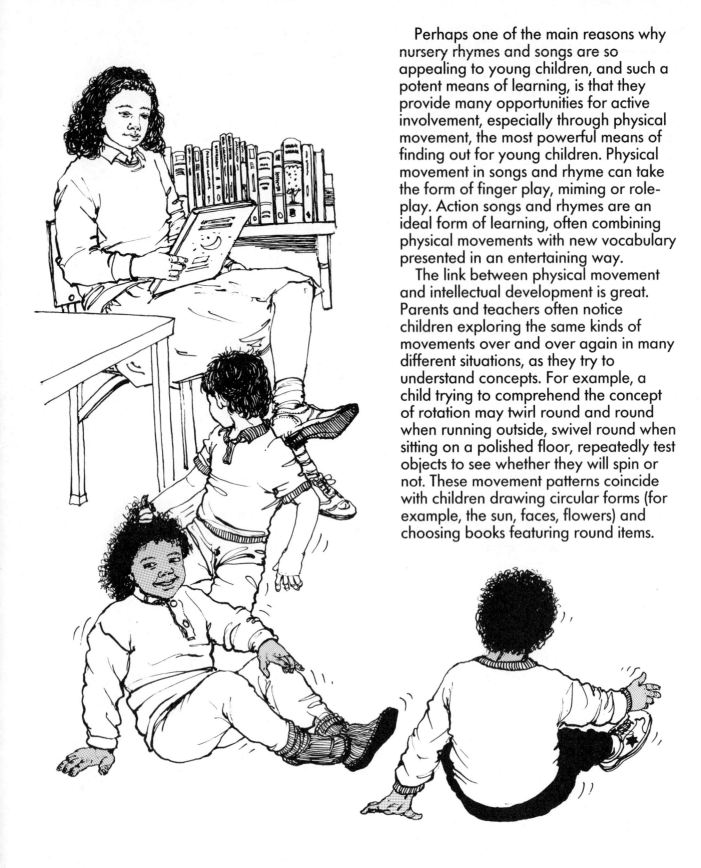

Perhaps one of the main reasons why nursery rhymes and songs are so appealing to young children, and such a potent means of learning, is that they provide many opportunities for active involvement, especially through physical movement, the most powerful means of finding out for young children. Physical movement in songs and rhyme can take the form of finger play, miming or role-play. Action songs and rhymes are an ideal form of learning, often combining physical movements with new vocabulary presented in an entertaining way.

The link between physical movement and intellectual development is great. Parents and teachers often notice children exploring the same kinds of movements over and over again in many different situations, as they try to understand concepts. For example, a child trying to comprehend the concept of rotation may twirl round and round when running outside, swivel round when sitting on a polished floor, repeatedly test objects to see whether they will spin or not. These movement patterns coincide with children drawing circular forms (for example, the sun, faces, flowers) and choosing books featuring round items.

These signs can show adults that a child may be working through a particular 'form of thought' (see *Extending Thought in Young Children – A Parent–Teacher Partnership*, by Chris Athey) or predominant learning interest. Athey categorises patterns of behaviour in children such as 'up and down', 'there and back', 'side by side', and 'round and round' and the concept of inside. A preoccupation with inside is frequently manifested in such behaviour as the child constantly wrapping things up or hiding them. Often, it can be these 'forms of thought' which exercise children's minds, when adults present an idea in a topic or a song and the child appears to latch on to a totally different aspect from that which the adult had in mind.

Adults can identify children's 'invisible wavelengths' of learning and become aware of them by carefully observing children's behaviour in different learning situations. A child can then be offered further ideas and opportunities related to his or her current 'form of thought'. An effective means of extending children's learning in this way is to offer a child a poem or song which fits in with the child's predominant interest. It is helpful, for example, to make a copy on card of particular songs and poems, cover them with transparent film, and store them in a box file for easy retrieval.

The poems and songs in this book may be used with groups, in topic work, and also with individual children to extend their 'forms of thought'. However, it is often found that individual interests spark off enthusiasm in others, either at the time, or at a later date. Athey, in *Extending Thought in Young Children – A Parent–Teacher Partnership* explains fully how children's learning can be greatly enhanced when parents and teachers work together to identify and nurture a full range of children's 'forms of thought'.

Rhymes and songs help children to develop concepts not only through physical movement, but also linguistically. Children extend their vocabulary, learn to pronounce new words, and have fun with language, as they experiment with rhyme, rhythm and repetition. Research has indicated the importance of being familiar with rhyme and alliteration to success in reading. Moreover, the words of favourite songs and poems make ideal material for shared reading. Songs and rhymes from other countries and cultures can add significantly to children's general knowledge and feelings of self-esteem and respect for others. Similarly, some rhymes from a bygone age can still be of value to children, as they can easily be updated or personalised to avoid cultural or sexual stereotyping. By reading this book, and trying out the activities suggested, early years' teachers may be encouraged to see nursery rhymes and songs in a new light.

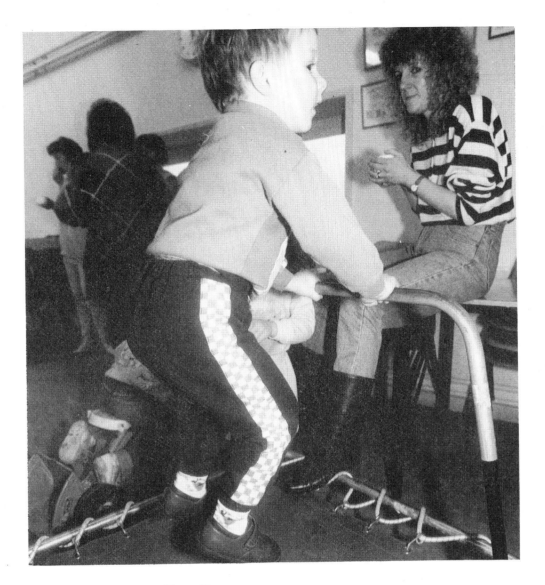

Up and down

Chapter one

The poems and songs in this chapter relate to children's interest in the motion of 'up and down'. Children explore these concepts in a variety of ways; for example, through climbing and jumping, and hand movements such as hammering.

Similarly, they are fascinated by how objects are moved up and down and how they balance, as well as phenomena both 'high up in the sky' and 'low down on the ground'.

Fire-fighters

Down the pole
Through the hole
Der . . . der . . . der . . . der
Der . . . der . . . der
Water on, hoses up – sszzz!
Ladder under window
Up and up I go.
Come with me and
Don't look down
'Til we touch the ground.

Linda Mort

One of the most vivid imaginary contexts for children's love of climbing up and down is that of fire-fighting. This poem is ideal for children to recite as they mime the actions. Discuss the fact that both men and women are fire-fighters. Show pictures of them sliding down a pole, and ask the children why they think this is done. Can the children think of any other activities involving climbing up and down, for example, slides? How do they sometimes feel at the top of a very high ladder and why must they hold on tight?

Climbing high

Objective
To develop problem-solving skills through structured play.

What you need
A slide or climbing frame with platform, a cardboard box, fabric, adhesive, scissors, string, a toy cat.

What to do
Transform a climbing frame or a slide into a 'real' fire-fighter's ladder in the following way. Take a cardboard box, roughly the width of the slide, and wedge it at the top of the ladder. The open end of the box should face the top of the ladder. (It may be necessary to tie it on with string. Use this method, too, to secure the box on to the platform of a climbing frame.) With the fabric, stick curtains on each side of the open box to make a window. Place a small toy cat in the window.

Discuss with the children why the cat needs to be rescued, for instance, did the house catch fire and, if so, why? – perhaps the cat was locked in the bathroom. Encourage the children to plan how they are going to carry the cat down, once they are at the top of the ladder. The cat may be frightened and may need something to secure it when it is being carried.

Up or down?

Objective
To develop the concepts of up and down through language and mime.

What you need
No special requirements.

What to do
If possible, arrange a visit to a fire station or a visit by a fire crew to your nursery or school. After the visit, explain that fire-fighters have to move up and down a lot in their job. Divide the class into two groups, the 'ups' and the 'downs'. Create simple sentences about fire-fighters' activities, using the words 'up' and 'down'. The relevant group then has to mime the action, for example, the fire-fighter pulls up her fire trousers, slides down the pole, rolls up the shutters on the fire-engine, climbs up the ladder, or beats down the grass fire with flame beaters etc.

Follow-up
The sentences can be written on a large sheet of paper to make a class poem for shared reading. Write the words 'up' and 'down' in two different colours.

Higher and higher

Objective
To develop the concept of height in relation to the use of ladders.

What you need
Construction kits to make ladders, for example, Mobilo, toy cars, pipe-cleaners, a doll's house, play people, or a real window cleaner, catalogues.

What to do
Talk about people who use ladders, such as window cleaners. If possible, invite a window cleaner to school for a chat. Let the children cut out pictures of different kinds of ladders from catalogues, to make a 'ladder book'. Tell them that the windows of the doll's house need cleaning. Can they make their own ladders from construction kits? How will they be carried on the toy cars? (Straps to secure them can be made from pipe-cleaners.) How should they place the ladders against the house so they are safe? Warn the children that they should never climb ladders, either at home or anywhere else.

Follow-up
Ask the children what happens when fire-fighters and window cleaners have to work on buildings which are too tall for ladders. Bring in pictures of fire-fighters' hydraulic cradles and window cleaners' cradles which are used on skyscrapers. (Some children may have their own hydraulic cradles on toy fire-engines, which are widely available.)

Jack-in-the-box

Jack-in-the-box jumps up like this.
He makes me laugh when he waggles his head.
I gently push him down again,
Saying 'Jack-in-the-box, you must go to bed'.

Traditional

This well-known poem delights children as it centres around their love of springing up to surprise someone. It also appeals to their pleasure in mimicking a reprimanding adult, wagging a finger in gentle rebuke at the 'child', Jack, who does not want to go to bed.

Knees bend

Objectives
To develop skills of co-operation and body awareness.

What you need
A large cardboard box, pictures of frogs or grasshoppers jumping.

What to do
Tell two children that they can take turns in being the 'Jack' and hiding in the box. How will each child fit inside? Using one child to demonstrate, show how the child must crouch down, and point out how the child's knees are 'folded' before they stretch out in the jump. Ask the children to stand straight and try jumping without first bending their knees. Can they do it? Ask them how they should stand to jump as high as possible. Show them pictures of how frogs and grasshoppers fold their legs before leaping into the air.

Let the children take turns to be either the 'grown-up' or Jack, who must jump up or crouch down depending on the 'grown-up's' instructions.

Zigzag fun

Objective
To explore folded shapes.

What you need
A concertina or squeeze box (if possible), fans, a pleated skirt, a pleated lampshade, a garden trellis, an old-fashioned 'concertina' camera, long, thick pipe-cleaners, paper, pencils, strips of card, sugar paper, adhesive, small boxes.

What to do
Bring in a collection of items which fold in a zigzag way. Show how they are small when folded, and large when stretched out. Let the children fold themselves up and then stretch out. Ask them to make a zigzag shape flat on the table, with a long, thick pipe-cleaner, then straighten it out again. Let them make another zigzag, stand it vertically, and then gently squash it.

Some children may enjoy drawing horizontal and vertical zigzag patterns. They could make simple Jack-in-the-boxes, using strips of folded card attached to a head and arms, and stuck inside a small box.

Spring time

Objective
To observe the action of springs.

What you need
A selection of Jack-in-the-boxes, including a broken one, springs, an old torch, coiled flexes, long, thick pipe-cleaners, push-down springy toys, a sprung garden chair, magazine pictures of sprung furniture, a pogo stick (if possible), *Tom's Cat* by Charlotte Voake.

What to do
Ask the children to bring in some Jack-in-the-boxes. Explain that they have to be stronger than the zigzag models made from card. Let the children feel the body of one of the Jacks, and look at the spring inside a broken one.

Ask the children to make a horizontal curvy zigzag, like a snake, from a long, thick pipe-cleaner. Ask them to stand it upright and squash it gently. What happens? Let the children examine push-down springy toys, such as frogs and 'jumping towers' etc.

Follow-up
Ask the children to think of where we can find springs at home and to bring in relevant magazine pictures (for example, mattresses, chairs, prams, large sprung toys). Bring in a sprung garden chair for the children to examine, and, if possible, a pogo stick. Read *Tom's Cat* to the class.

The blacksmith

'Robert Barnes, blacksmith fine,
Can you shoe this horse of mine?'
'Yes, indeed, as you will tell,
I can do it very well.
There's a nail and there's a prod,
And now, you see, your horse is shod.'

Traditional

From babyhood, children love to experiment with hammering, initially to delight in the sounds, and later as they try to 'mend' things. This traditional poem, written before the invention of cars, still has value for today's children. It introduces them to a wide area of general knowledge and technological skills. Horses still have to be shod, and a visit to a blacksmith's or a wrought-iron worker's forge is exciting. If you substitute each child's name for 'Robert Barnes', the poem becomes personal, and children will be encouraged to think of female blacksmiths, mechanics or engineers.

especially after a visit to a real blacksmith's forge. If this is not possible, they could be shown a short video film of what happens in a blacksmith's forge. Using some card, cut out four horseshoes about the size of the soles of the rocking horse's feet. Punch three holes in each shoe. Stick some Blu-Tack to the soles. The horse is now ready. Let children take turns to be the blacksmith and the customers (farmers and jockeys, for example) bringing their horses to be shod. The blacksmith taps the plastic pegs through the holes in the card into the Blu-Tack under the soles.

Follow-up
Take apart an old shoe, and show how small nails are used around the heel area. Take the children to visit a shoe repairer. Explain that although the soles are usually repaired with adhesive, heels are still tapped into place with small nails, or staples from a staple gun machine.

Rocking horse forge

Objective
To introduce children to real applications of hammering.

What you need
A rocking horse, Blu-Tack, card, scissors, a pencil, a hole punch, plastic pegs from peg boards, a toy hammer, an old shoe.

What to do
Children enjoy 'shoeing' a rocking horse,

Ask what sort of different jobs Peter/ Paula might be doing, for example, hammering out dents on a car, testing for reflexes, plumbing, repairing a fence. If there is a wooden fence nearby, let the children see how many nails they can spot.

In the classroom, provide wood, nails and hammers alongside all the other 'fixing' resources such as adhesive, sticky tape, staples, string, split pins, needle and cotton. Through discussion, help children to plan and choose the most appropriate materials and methods to put various objects together.

Do it yourself

Objective
To provide opportunities for children to develop hammering skills in a CDT context.

What you need
Wood, nails, hammers, hammering toys, for example, pegs and bench, picture hammering games, a medical set.

What to do
Arrange a visit from a carpenter, caretaker or parent who is a DIY enthusiast, to show the children a range of hammers, mallets and nails. (Stress to the children that they should never touch these without an adult being present.) Sing the song 'Peter [Paula] hammers':

Peter hammers with one hammer,
One hammer, one hammer,
Peter hammers with one hammer,
All day long.

Peter hammers with two hammers,
[etc].

Musical hammers

Objective
To develop listening skills and a sense of rhythm.

What you need
Instruments which require 'beaters', for example, drums, piano, glockenspiel, chime bars, coconut shells.

What to do
Ask the children whether a blacksmith hammers in the horseshoe gently or fiercely, and why. Let the children pretend to hammer in the horseshoe gently, using one of the instruments, and then fiercely, as they beat out the shape. Can a child beat out the poem without words, softly and loudly, slowly and quickly? Introduce the coconut shells and let children make the sounds of gentle trotting, fierce galloping, and so on.

Follow-up
Open up a piano and let the children see the hammers.

One, two, three, four, five

One, two, three, four, five,
Once I caught a fish alive.
Six, seven, eight, nine, ten,
Then I let it go again.
Why did you let it go?
Because it bit my finger so.
Which finger did it bite?
This little finger on my right.

Traditional

This well-known, catchy song is always popular with children. As well as being valuable for teaching number names, it can also lead to an enjoyable exploration of a fascination for picking things up and releasing them, at arm's length, using various devices.

Let's go fishing

Objectives
To explore magnetism and to develop number recognition.

What you need
Fishing tackle, a magnet, string, garden canes, paper-clips, card, scissors, felt-tipped pens, a clock timer.

What to do
If possible, arrange for a fishing enthusiast to visit school, to show hooks, baits and nets that he or she uses. Make a magnetic fishing game with the children. Many children will have seen the type that can be bought in shops. Use their descriptions to involve them in making the game, for instance in drawing and cutting out the fish. Make pairs of fish with each number from one to ten. The object of the game is for the pair of children to co-operate and to 'beat the clock', in other words to collect ten fish each in a row numbered one to ten within ten minutes. As they collect and arrange their fish, they should help each other by swapping any numbers they already have.

How can we do that?

Objective
To introduce practical problem-solving skills.

What you need
A child's fishing net, a dustpan, a long-handled dustpan, a chair trolley (if possible), a mechanical hand 'grabber', a feather duster, a bamboo cane, a duster, elastic bands, a torch, magnets, sponges.

What to do
Children are intrigued by devices which help people move objects up and down. Give them a child's fishing net and ask them for ideas for a simple game (for instance, to see who can 'net' and lift up the most small bricks from a cardboard box). Show the children a dustpan and a long-handled version, and ask them how they differ. If possible, let the children see how a chair trolley lifts chairs slightly, and wheels them away.

Show the children a disabled person's mechanical hand 'grabber', and a picture of a litter collector using a spiked stick. Can the children think of any problems they would like to help solve, and have they any ideas for types of aids? Show them a feather duster and provide a bamboo cane, together with a duster, elastic bands, sponges, torch, magnets, and so on, to set them thinking.

Up and down day

Objective
To develop structural and shared reading skills.

What you need
Pictures of fishing boats and cargo ships, pictures and/or models of the following: cranes, tipper trucks, fork-lift trucks, bulldozers, a car ramp, a garage lift, a breakdown vehicle; card, felt-tipped pens, sugar paper, staples.

What to do
Most children are interested in all kinds of mechanical lifting devices. Show them a picture of a large fishing boat with a crane device for lifting nets of fish. Also show pictures of cargo ships loading and unloading containers with cranes.

Have an 'up and down' day when children bring toys from home which go up and down, for example, toy cranes or tipper trucks. In front of each object, write a card saying, 'the ramp goes up and down'; 'the fork-lift truck goes up and down'. Read these with the children. Ask the children each to draw a picture of their toy and then stick the card underneath. Make the pictures into a large class book for shared reading.

See-saw Margery Daw

See-saw Margery Daw,
You're in the air and I'm on the floor.
Now I go up and you go down,
Then it's my turn on the ground.
Goodness gracious, well I never!
I think this could last for ever!

Traditional

This is a fun alternative to the original rhyme. For maximum effect it is best said slowly by one child at a time, with an adult's help, as children play on a see-saw. When one child has said it, the adult should go over to the other child and say it with her. Alternatively, it can be sung, using the traditional tune for the first line, and repeating this line throughout. Ask the children whether they think a see-saw ride could last for ever and if not, why.

mentioning one bucket of sand. Explain that the giant decided to make two cakes, and that each cake must use exactly one bucketful of sand, 'not one bit more, nor one bit less'. Show the children that the giant has already filled one bucket with sand and, to be absolutely correct, has decided to weigh the other bucket, so that it not only looks the same, but weighs the same, too. Tie the full bucket to one end of the see-saw, and the empty bucket to the other end. Using words such as 'heavy, light, getting heavier', let the children take turns to fill the empty bucket until the see-saw balances.

The giant's scales

Objective
To develop the concepts of heavy, light and balance.

What you need
Kitchen balance scales, a see-saw, two buckets, string, dry sand, sugar paper, felt-tipped pens, a stapler.

What to do
Show the children some kitchen balance scales and talk about how they are used to weigh ingredients in cooking. Make up a story about a giant who loved eating sand cake. Make a 'recipe' book, and read the recipe to the children,

Moving see-saw picture

Objectives
To develop concepts of up and down, and co-operation skills.

What you need
Paper or card, scissors, a pencil, crayons, a brass split pin, sticky tape.

What to do
Ask a child to draw a see-saw, starting with a triangle shape for the see-saw pivot. The child can then cut out a long rectangle for the seat, and with help fix it in place with a brass split pin through the paper. Now the child can draw small pictures of himself and a friend, cut them out and stick them with sticky tape on to each end of the see-saw. The two children can then gently hold each end of the see-saw and sing the song, moving the picture up and down appropriately.

Weighing up

Objective
To develop skills of prediction.

What you need
Balance scales, small toys and objects.

What to do
Place a small toy in one of the pans of the scales, then bring out another toy and ask, 'If I put this in the other pan, will it stay up, go down or balance?' After some demonstrations, ask the children to imagine some giant-sized balance scales and to think about well-known cartoon characters sitting in them, for instance, if Tom the cat sat in this pan, and Jerry came along, would Jerry's pan stay up, go down, or balance? Other pairs are Yogi Bear and Boo Boo, Postman Pat and Jess, Mickey and Minnie Mouse. Let children take turns at asking the questions.

Humming-bird

Humming-bird, humming-bird, why don't you hum?
I do not hum because I am dumb.
Then why are you called humming-bird of all things?
Because of the noise I make with my wings.

Humming-bird, humming-bird, humming-bird, humming-bird,
Humming-bird, humming-bird, why don't you hum?
Humming-bird, humming-bird, humming-bird, humming-bird,
Humming-bird, humming-bird, why don't you hum?

Odette Thomas

Children have a keen interest in all aspects of flight, whether natural or engine-powered. This Jamaican song appeals to children because of its direct language; it has just the sort of question which children are likely to ask birds, animals, vehicles etc. Discuss with the children other birds and creatures who fly high and then come down looking for worms, insects, and pollen.

Flower dance

Objective
To develop an understanding of how birds and bees collect nectar or pollen from flowers.

What you need
Sugar paper, scissors, yellow gummed paper, a felt-tipped pen, white paper, a tambour, sleigh bells.

What to do
Using sugar paper, cut out six large flower heads with petals and spread them out on a large floor space. Cut out small circles from yellow gummed paper (one for each child) and scatter some on each flower. On a large piece of white paper, draw either a nest with some baby humming-birds or a beehive, and place it in the middle of the floor. Ask the children to pretend to be either humming-birds collecting nectar, or bees collecting pollen. Explain that it is a rainy day and that the birds and bees can collect nectar and pollen only when the sun comes out. In small groups, the children should dance around the flowers 'in the rain' as you drum on a tambour with your fingertips. As soon as you shake the sleigh bells (the sun) the children must fly to a flower, take some nectar or pollen (one piece of yellow paper) and drop it in the nest or hive. This should be continued until all the children have had a turn.

Bird's eye view

Objective
To develop observational skills.

What you need
A tray, breadcrumbs, a plastic washing basket, a toy car, paper, a felt-tipped pen, a stool, *Up and Up* by Shirley Hughes.

What to do
Draw six separate pictures of the side view and aerial view of a bird table, a washing basket and a car. Tell the children that when birds fly they view everything from the top, not the side.

Let individual children lie face downwards on a stool, and pretend to fly like a bird. Place a tray with breadcrumbs (to represent an aerial view of a bird table), the washing basket and the toy car, one at a time underneath the child's face and ask the child to look carefully at them. When the child stands up, give her the pictures and see if she can match each side view to its aerial view, and say what they are.

Follow-up
Read *Up and Up* to the children.

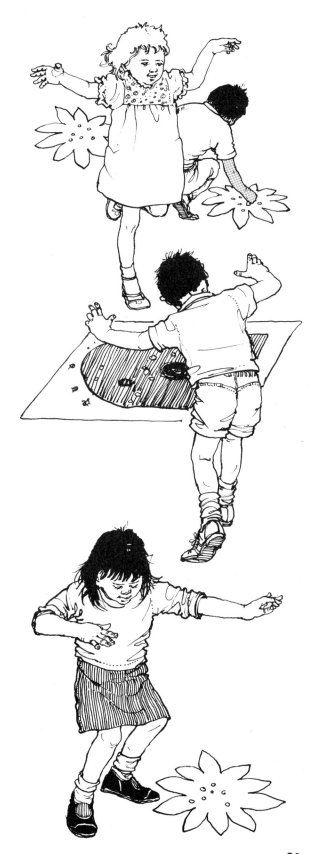

High and low trails

Objective
To explore aspects of height and direction through trails.

What you need
A soft toothbrush, a lolly stick, an elastic band, paper, paint in an open margarine pot, a kite, crêpe paper, Plasticine, invisible thread, sticky tape.

What to do
Many children are fascinated to see aeroplane contrails in the sky, and will enjoy making 'aeroplane trail' pictures. Take a soft toothbrush and with the aid of an elastic band help a child to fix a lolly stick at right angles towards one end of the brush. The stick forms the 'wings'. The child then dips the brush in the paint and pushes the 'aeroplane' across the paper sky, brush-side down, leaving contrails behind it.

Some children may notice car exhaust fumes and snails' trails. Let the children make a Plasticine snail and wrap some invisible thread around it. Secure one end of the thread to a corner of the table with sticky tape and, starting at that same corner, let the children 'walk' their snail across the table, leaving its 'trail' behind.

Follow up
For 'high trails' make streamers from strips of rolled-up crêpe paper which children can run with. Let the children watch a kite flying. To create 'low trails', a child can drop stones on a walk across grass and hide some treasure. Another child then has to follow the trails to find the treasure. This can also be done in winter, following a footprint trail in the snow.

There and back

Chapter two

There are endless possibilities for exploring the theme of 'there and back': rocking, swinging, moving in different ways, carrying items from place to place, or riding in a vehicle. As children recite or sing the poems and songs given in this chapter, and carry out the suggested actions and movement, often in role-play, they are also exploring aspects of speed, direction, stopping and starting, in a variety of scientific, mathematical and imaginary contexts.

Two little boats

Two little boats are on the sea,
All is calm as calm can be.
Gently the wind begins to blow,
Two little boats rock to and fro.
Loudly the wind begins to shout,
Two little boats are tossed about.
Gone is the wind, the storm, the rain,
Two little boats sail on again.

Author unknown

Rocking is the most basic form of 'there and back' movement, and is loved by all young children. This poem is ideal for extending an enjoyment of and interest in rocking into something more scientific, as it introduces children to an understanding of how the wind causes waves. Let the children sit in pairs on the floor holding hands, and making themselves into 'boats', rocking forwards and backwards.

boat on the water and let one child at a time pretend to be the wind. Each child can make the boat move forwards by gently blowing down a straw, and backwards by sucking up the straw or 'blowing backwards'. Talk about how the wind blows the water and the boat 'to and fro', as in the poem. Each boat should last just long enough for each child's turn.

Follow-up
Let the children use their whole bodies as waves, running forwards and backwards. Excellent wave patterns can be made with small rollers in paint. Can some of the children talk about items washed up on the seashore, such as shells, seaweed, bottles, treasure chests? Read *Come Away from the Water, Shirley.*

Blow the boats

Objective
To develop an understanding of the effect of wind on water.

What you need
One rectangular plastic ice-cream carton, water, paper, scissors, straws, pencils, paint, rollers, *Come Away from the Water, Shirley* by John Burningham.

What to do
Cut a small piece of paper into the shape shown. Fold the bottom rectangle upwards, to make a very simple boat. Fill the plastic carton with water, place the

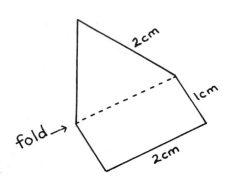

Rock-a-bye teddy

Objective
To foster CDT skills while making a miniature hammock.

What you need
A small teddy bear, cloth, a needle, cotton, scissors, two suction hooks (optional), string, a baby's swinging crib (if possible), *Meg at Sea* by Helen Nicholl and Jan Pienkowski.

What to do
Talk about how sailors sometimes sleep in hammocks. Let the children make a swinging hammock motion with their arms. Point out that hammocks swing from side to side, not backwards and forwards.

Older children may like to make a hammock for a favourite teddy or doll. Depending on the children's capabilities, offer as much or as little help as needed to make their hammocks. Discuss the length of fabric required by measuring the teddy against it. Most will need to have the cloth cut for them. Older children may be able to sew a wide hem at the top and bottom. Thread the string through the hems in two loops. The hammock may be suspended in a corner using the suction hooks, or, alternatively between two chairs.

Follow-up
Read *Meg at Sea* and ask the children about any time they have been seasick. Sing 'Rock-a-bye baby', and ask whether the children think it is a good idea to hang a cradle from a tree.

Teddy's accident

Objectives
To encourage asking questions and to foster emergent writing.

What you need
An easel, a teddy bear, bandages, plasters, paper or card, scissors, felt-tipped pens, pencils, crayons, pictures of rocking and swinging toys, curved bricks, small toys, construction kits.

What to do
Put bandages and plasters on a teddy bear. Settle the children and sit yourself behind an easel so you cannot be seen. Let the teddy appear above the easel and introduce himself. Let Teddy say to the children, 'Can you ask me some questions to find out what happened to me?' Encourage the children's questions so that a story emerges along the lines of how Teddy didn't listen to his mum who had told him not to stand up on his rocking horse, and how he had to go to hospital.

Let the children make get-well cards for him, using their own levels of emergent writing.

If children walk around the room looking down at their feet as they say this poem, they become particularly aware of how, in order to move, they must put one foot 'in front of the other'. Ask the children to show you what happens when they put one leg behind the other.

Teach them the meaning of the word 'stile', by building a low stile from large bricks. The children can jump over it as they play some of the walking games suggested below. The towns of London and Dover can, of course, be substituted by local names.

Don't fall off!

Objective
To develop body and spatial awareness in relation to balance.

What you need
Benches or a balance bar, a skipping rope, a toy umbrella (optional), rubber mats, platform boxes, circus-type dressing up clothes, thick paper, scissors.

What to do
All children go through the stage of being delighted when they find they can walk along the top of a low garden wall by themselves or by holding an adult's hand. Show the children pictures of tightrope walkers and let them dress up accordingly. Let each child pretend to be a tightrope walker by walking along a skipping rope laid on the ground. For more realism, raise a bench or balance bar a few inches off the ground, by resting it at each end on wide platform boxes. Place mats underneath the bench and let the 'tightrope walkers' walk across, perhaps to the accompaniment of appropriate music.

Tickling teddy bears

Objectives
To develop social and oral skills through work in pairs.

What you need
Cards, crayons, pencils, scissors.

What to do
Ask the children to put one finger in front of the other, and 'walk' them across the table. Now ask them to do it quickly. What does it remind them of? — tickling!

Let the children make card teddy bears with two finger holes. When each child has a 'tickling teddy', let them sit in pairs and play 'Round and round the garden' with one another.

Follow-up
Ask the children to put one knee in front of the other on the floor, and then realise that they are crawling. Just for fun, as they crawl, can they try and put one elbow in front of the other, too?

Different walks

Objective
To develop feelings of empathy through music and movement.

What you need
Outline drawings of a duck, a soldier, a giant, a ballet dancer, a cat, a person with a heavily bandaged leg, an angry-looking child, suitable 'walking' music.

What to do
Discuss with the children different ways of walking; for example, how a duck waddles, a soldier marches, a giant strides, a ballet-dancer tiptoes, a cat creeps, a person with an injured leg limps, and a bad-tempered child stamps. Play the music and hold up the pictures one at a time. With each picture the children must adopt a suitable walk. Let them try these different walks both forwards and backwards.

Slowly, slowly

Slowly, slowly, very slowly
Creeps the garden snail.
Slowly, slowly, very slowly
Up the wooden rail.

Quickly, quickly, very quickly
Runs the little mouse.
Quickly, quickly, very quickly
Round about the house.

Author unknown

'Slowly, slowly' is a very simple rhyme which focuses on children's growing awareness of speed. Once the children are familiar with the words, they will enjoy saying the first half slowly and the second half as quickly as possible. Ask the children to think of other animals which move quickly and slowly (for instance, grasshoppers and elephants), or vehicles (such as steamrollers and racing cars). Can the children think of why a mouse, in particular, would need to run quickly around a house?

Action replay and fast-forward

Objective
To encourage children to think about the sequence of physical movements, and the consequences of rushing.

What you need
A video recorder, a clip of a video film showing a football 'action replay', any other suitable non-football film, a record player, a metronome, an electronic keyboard.

What to do
Show a clip of a football match which is followed by an 'action replay'. Ask the children to close their eyes and think carefully about what they need to do to kick a football. Ask them to pretend to be an amazing snail who can play football. How would it kick the ball? Then let them show you, in slow motion. Other ideas for activities to try in slow motion are walking, getting dressed, brushing teeth and making a phone call.

Now show a clip of another, non-football film, first at normal speed, then using the fast-forward button. Ask the children to close their eyes and imagine themselves washing their faces at normal speed. Tell them that the mouse in the poem sometimes rushes too much and has accidents. Let them show you how the mouse might wash its face at fast-forward speed. Ask what might go wrong if they really washed at that speed (for instance, water might gush out and cause a flood, they might get soap in their eyes, they might not rinse and dry properly and get a sore face). Let the children show you other fast-forward actions.

garden canes. Take the snail cane and very slowly point to each word of the first verse, as the children say the words with you. The children must say the word only when you point to it. Choose different children to be the 'slow snail' and point to the words, while the rest read. For the second verse, take the mouse cane and point ot the words (relatively) quickly.

Follow-up
Duplicate the poem and send it home to parents with instructions for 'slow and fast' shared reading.

Follow-up
Help the children to say nursery rhymes very quickly and very slowly. Introduce a few simple tongue-twisters. Bring in a metronome, and an electronic keyboard which can play a tune quickly or slowly.

Slow, slow, quick, quick, slow

Objective
To develop early reading skills.

What you need
Large sheets of paper, felt-tipped pens, card, two garden canes, sticky tape, a duplicated letter home.

What to do
Write out 'Slowly, slowly' on large sheets of paper and attach them to the wall. Draw a snail and a mouse on card, cut them out and stick them to the top of the

Speedometer

Objectives
To develop an understanding of different speeds and number recognition.

What you need
A large piece of card, large split pin(s), an easel, felt-tipped pens.

What to do
On the large piece of card, draw a large fan shape. The card should fit on to an easel. With a felt-tipped pen, write in the numbers 0 to 100 in tens, as on a car speedometer. Make a card pointer and fix it to the speedometer with split pins. Talk to the children about different speeds used by vehicles when they are moving off, slowing down, and so on. Discuss the use of the accelerator pedal.

Let the children move around the room, changing speed in 'miles per hour', as you call out increasingly large numbers, for instance '10 miles an hour, 20, 30', and conversely, as they slow down and lose speed. Some children may be able to take your place and give out instructions.

Lollipop lady

**Lollipop lady,
lollipop lady,
wave your magic stick
and make the traffic
stop a while
so we can cross the street.**

John Agard

A road safety theme is always popular in nurseries and reception classes, as well as being a vital part of young children's education. This poem is ideal as a follow-up to seeing a lollipop person at work. One aspect which many children will seize upon is the idea of 'stopping' and, in particular, the feeling of authority in making traffic and people stop or go.

If it is possible to arrange for a lollipop person to visit the children, they will no doubt enjoy the chance of holding the stick, perhaps with a little help. Ask the children if it is a magic stick, and, if not, then how does it make the traffic stop?

STOP!

Objective
To develop stopping skills through structured play.

What you need
Sit'n'ride cars, kitchen roll tubes, a white shirt, sticky tape, a lollipop person's cap, fluorescent arm bands, toy cars, play people, a lollipop stick, card, felt-tipped pens, paper, adhesive, a computer turtle or 'roamer', remote-control toys, a police hat.

What to do
Arrange for an outdoor structured play session with the theme of a busy street, in which adults and children share the roles of the lollipop person, pedestrian children and drivers. Make a lollipop stick from kitchen roll tubes, card and paint. Much valuable conversation will emerge about 'stopping, starting, walking quickly, not running and the green cross code'. This can also be done indoors with fewer children, and/or in the block play area, with toy cars and play people.

Follow-up
Let children take turns to wear the police hat and pretend to be on traffic duty while a group of children move round as traffic obeying the policeman or -woman's signal to stop and start. Children will also benefit from exploring the 'stop, go' function on a turtle linked to a computer, or by using remote-control toys.

Crash landings

Objective
To investigate impact.

What you need
Toy cars, large bricks, a road mat, small bricks, play people, a water tray, rulers, sticky tape.

What to do
The previous activities emphasise developing children's awareness about being able to stop in time. The opposite event, the crash, or impact, holds an equal fascination for children. This is evident in their experiments with crashing toy cars into skirting boards and furniture, or in 'splash' activities in water play.

Arrange some crashing activities with toy cars and bricks so that children can explore the effects of speed on the size of crashes. Include play people, ambulances, hospital buildings and other emergency services. At the water tray, rig up a simple diving board using rulers and sticky tape and let the children find out about the height of dives in relation to splash sizes.

Follow-up
Make up very simple poems about the effects of various things crashing, for example:

hands crash — clap!
people crash — bump!
lips crash — kiss!
little girl and water crash — splash!

Let the children explore a 'backwards crash' by playing 'Hands, knees and bumpsadaisy'.

Ready, steady, go!

Objectives
To develop listening skills and speedy reactions.

What you need
Toy cars, including two 'pull-backs' if possible, two wooden dowel rods, paper, felt-tipped pens, sticky tape.

What to do
Play some very simple races, using home-made 'start' and 'finish' flags, with the children as racing cars, or use toy cars. Put more emphasis on the fun and anticipation of starting correctly (no false starts or jumping the gun!), than on who wins. Listening skills can also be fostered by the ever-popular 'traffic lights' game, in which the children run around the room as traffic, reacting to the teacher's shouts of red, amber or green.

One morning

One morning the little boy woke up,
Got out of bed
And said to his mummy,
'I'm going for a walk.'

He went down the garden path
and shut the gate – SLAM!

He went down the road until he
came to a bridge.
He walked across the bridge – TRIP TRAP.

And he walked along the road 'til he
came to a river.
He looked up the river and down the river.
There was no bridge so he swam – SPLISH SPLASH.

When he got to the other side he walked
in the forest 'til he came to a
great big tree.

He looked round this side of the tree,
And he looked round that side of the tree,
But there was nothing there.
Then he heard a voice – TIGERS!

He ran through the forest –
He swam across the river –
He ran across the bridge –
He shut the gate . . . SLAM –
He ran in to his mother –
'Mummy', he said,
'I'm home!'

Author unknown; adapted Linda Mort

The theme of this poem, a little boy's desire for independence, a scary meeting, and a quick get-away back to the safety of home, is one with which many children will identify. The last verse (which should, of course, be read quickly), is about his return journey.

When the children have heard the poem, repeat the landmarks of the little boy's outward trip – the garden path, the gate, bridge, river and forest – and then see if any children can remember the landmarks in reverse order.

There and back

Objective
To describe routes there and back.

What you need
Bricks, play people, model tigers, blue paper, an easel, felt-tipped pens, white paper, toy cars, *Bears in the Night* by Stan and Jan Berenstain.

What to do
As you recite the poem with the children, draw the 'landmarks' on a sheet of paper attached to an easel. By the end of the poem you should have a simple plan of the little boy's route. Move the easel to the block area and, with a group of children, recreate the route using blue paper for the river, upright blocks for the forest, and so on. Encourage the children to look at the plan as they work.

Now let individual children take a play figure (the little boy), and walk it through the model, repeating key phrases. Let other children have a tiger each. As they creep forward, the first child quickly retraces the boy's steps, with all the children joining in the words.

Follow-up
With the children's help make a simple, roofless model of the nursery or school building, and using a play figure let the children talk through their route to class each morning — for instance, 'Through the entrance, into the car park, up the path to the front door, along the corridor and into our room!' The route could then be drawn out on paper. See if the children can talk through their homeward route.

Read *Bears in the Night*, which contains a scary, thrilling experience and a speedy escape, similar to the one in the poem.

Backwards and forwards

Objective
To explore the concept of being in reverse.

What you need
A square plastic mirror, a video recorder, a clip of suitable film.

What to do
Play the game 'What time is it, Mr Wolf' with a small group in plenty of space. Explain that sometimes, if we are frightened, we may try to move backwards, instead of turning round and running forwards. Play the game a second time, and let the children try escaping backwards.

Act out the forest incident in the poem. Some children can spread their arms and be trees, while others can be tigers. Make sure you have plenty of space. When the 'tigers' appear, let the 'little boy' try to move backwards out of the forest. Can the children explain why he keeps bumping into the trees?

Now let the children be car drivers, driving in reverse. Should they drive quickly or slowly? Why? How can real drivers see where they are going? Let about four children be trees, and give one 'driver' a square plastic mirror as she moves backwards. Let her see if she can avoid bumping into the trees.

Follow-up

Show a short clip from a video film, using rewind, and let the children try walking or pretending to go upstairs backwards.

Play the game of opposites in which you suggest an action, and the child must do the opposite (that is, the action in reverse), for example, 'Get out of bed, shut the gate, swim forwards, stand up, push your sock down, put your coat on, zip up your coat'.

Back-to-front

Objective

To encourage language and concept development through word play.

What you need

Fifteen Ways to Go to Bed by Kathy Henderson.

What to do

A further development of reversibility is the idea of 'back to front'. Take phrases from the poem, and see if the children can repeat them 'back to front', for instance little boy, garden path, trip trap, splish splash. The children will enjoy saying their names back to front, and reception children in particular will enjoy having the register taken occasionally with their names read out in reverse order.

Follow-up

Read 'Sam Smith', a story about a boy who sleeps with his feet on his pillow and his head at the end of the bed, in *Fifteen Ways to Go to Bed*.

The muffin man

Have you seen the muffin man?
The muffin man, the muffin man,
Oh, have you seen the muffin man,
Who lives down Drury Lane?

Oh yes, I've seen the muffin man,
The muffin man, the muffin man.
Oh yes, I've seen the muffin man,
Who lives down Drury Lane.

Traditional

This is a delightful old favourite, much loved by children. It can become even more enjoyable when some real muffins are brought in to sample. As well as enjoying the song in its traditional form, the children can also update the words. Simply replace 'muffin man' with 'dustbin man', 'postwoman', 'bus driver' or 'policewoman'. 'Who lives down Drury Lane' can be replaced by 'Who lives down our street/road'.

Flag-days

Objective
To develop early shopping skills in role-play.

What you need
A plastic tray with handles, belts, very small sticky labels or 'dots', felt-tipped pens, sticky tape, a tall tin can, paper, duplicated letters to parents, 'pretend' ice-cream and lollies, a torch.

What to do
Thread belts through the handles of a tray and put it on a child who is to be the 'muffin man'. He can 'sell' real muffins or models made from salt pastry.

Hold a week of flag-days. Send a letter home saying that you would like to raise a little money for your nursery or school charity by letting the children have their own flag-days. Ask each parent to send in five separate pennies in an envelope. Label a tin with the name of your charity. Cover the top with card which has a slit in it. Place the 'flags' or, in this case, sticky labels on the tray and give it to the first 'flagseller'. As each child has five pennies to spend at different times, it will be possible for every child to be a 'seller' during the course of the week. For a class of 30, have six 'sellers' a day, one at a time, each selling to four different children. Although 150 stickers or dots will be needed to allow each child to buy one each day, the smallest size are inexpensive, especially if bought on a roll.

Have you seen the music man?

Objective
To develop creative problem-solving skills.

What you need
A picture of a one-man band or busker, percussion instruments, belts, ribbons, string, squeakers and other small noise-makers, elastic bands, a boiler suit, a baby carrier, items of uniform, scarves, dolls.

What to do
Continue the theme of carrying items on the body into the area of music-making by changing the words 'muffin man' to 'music boy' or 'music girl'. Ask one child to choose a percussion instrument and hold it still. The rest of the group sing, changing the last line to 'she plays a tambourine' (or whatever instrument the child has chosen), after which the child plays, then chooses another child.

Next, show the children pictures of a one-man band, and let them suggest ideas for fastening instruments on to different parts of their body so they will still play. They will, of course, need your help to put their ideas into practice, by tying the instruments in the places they suggest. Buy a few round plastic squeakers or other small noise makers. Great fun can be had from some ingenious ideas of the chldren such as attaching a squeaker to the bottom of a shoe with a strong elastic band, or tying a squeaker under an arm.

Follow-up
Bring in clothes specially designed to carry things, for example, a boiler suit with several pockets, a uniform shirt with epaulettes to carry gloves, a money belt or pouch. Also, bring in a baby carrier and show the children how it is used. Let the children experiment by making their own, using scarves and, dolls, with your help.

Stop me and buy one

Objective
To encourage imaginative structured play.

What you need
A pedal car, or large sit'n'ride vehicle, cardboard boxes, a toddle truck, a wheelbarrow, coloured sugar paper, packaging tape, card, salt pastry, cotton wool, lolly sticks, felt-tipped pens, white shirts and caps, plastic milk bottles or cartons.

What to do
When the children are familiar with the song, talk about mobile food sellers who are seen today, such as sellers of hot-dogs, baked potatoes, chestnuts, ice-cream and popcorn. The children can become mobile food vendors by dressing up in a white coat and pushing a wheelbarrow containing their wares, perhaps made from salt pastry.

Probably the most popular sort of mobile food seller is the ice-cream van. Make some pretend ice-creams from coloured sugar paper. Sit a child in a pedal car and place a very large upturned cardboard box, which has a large window cut in one side, over the child's head. The box may be temporarily secured on to the car with tape.

Can the children suggest ways of making a milk float? (perhaps by tying a pedal car to a toddle truck filled with plastic milk bottles or cartons). The following rhyme from Jamaica may encourage those who have milk delivered to find out who does their milk round:
Every morning at six o'clock
Ma Dookie bring the milk
She comes in front and shouts 'oo-oo'
And then she cries 'mil-lik'.

(Odette Thomas)

Side by side

Chapter three

Research by Piaget and others has revealed that children's mathematical concepts are based on their physical exploration of shape, position and size. Many mathematical concepts can be learned actively through floor play in the classroom block area, by means of enjoyable, open-ended structured play situations. These give a child opportunities for physical movement, use of imagination and problem-solving.

The poems and songs in this chapter have been chosen to help teachers develop and extend children's interest in hiding objects in different positions, covering space with separate items in sequence, joining up objects, co-operating with one another, and matching and counting objects.

Teddy bear

Teddy lost his coat,
Teddy lost his hat,
Teddy lost his rubber boots –
What do you think of that?

Teddy found his coat,
Teddy found his hat,
Teddy found his rubber boots –
He'd left them on the mat!

Author unknown

This poem deals with the common problem of lost belongings, but it does have a happy ending. Children are reassured to find out that they are not the only ones who lose things. The poem can be varied if children think of other items for teddy to lose, and alternative places to find them.

Where did I put it?

Objective
To develop an understanding of prepositions.

What you need
A teddy bear, a doormat, a pair of toddlers' wellington boots, a coat and hat, bricks, planks, sheets of paper, a felt-tipped pen.

What to do
Ask the children for ideas about where teddy might look for his belongings; for instance, under the table, behind the settee, on top of the chest of drawers. Write down these ideas on a large piece of paper, and put it on the wall or on an easel, next to the block area. Let the children build the furniture items from bricks and planks. Place the doormat with teddy's wellington boots, coat and hat on it in a far corner. Let each child pretend to be a parent, helping teddy to find his clothes by telling him to look 'under the table' and elsewhere in the room. Another child can 'walk' the teddy.

Where's teddy?

Objective
To develop story-making skills.

What you need
A copy of *Where's Spot?* by Eric Hill, sugar paper, crayons, felt-tipped pens, scissors, sticky tape.

What to do
Read the story of *Where's Spot?* Tell the children that sometimes teddy's mum can't find him. See if the children can make up a very simple story in which mum looks in perhaps two different places before finding him. Using the child's phrases, make a simple four-page book from a folded piece of paper, with flaps attached with sticky tape.

Where does it go?

Objective
To develop concepts of a set.

What you need
A doll's house, household objects such as a fork, a toothbrush, and an empty milk carton.

What to do
Ask the children where teddy should really have put his clothes instead of leaving them on the mat. Bring in a collection of household objects and see if the children can place them in the correct rooms of the doll's house.

Early in the morning

Come down to the station early in the morning,
See all the railway trains standing in a row.
See all the drivers starting up the engines,
Clickety click and clickety clack,
Off they go!

Come down to the garage early in the morning,
See all the buses standing in a row.
See all the drivers starting up the engines,
Rumble, rumble, rumble, rumble,
Off they go!

Come down to the seaside early in the morning,
See all the motor-boats floating in a row.
See all the drivers starting up the engines,
Splishing, splishing, sploshing, sploshing,
Off they go!

Come down to the airport early in the morning,
See all the aeroplanes standing in a row.
See all the pilots starting up the engines,
Whirring, whirring, whirring, whirring,
Off they go!

Traditional

Children enjoy floor play in which they cover space using separate objects in rows, either 'side by side' or 'end to end'. This poem is an ideal stimulus to such play, especially if the children have previously visited some of the places mentioned in the poem. Ask the children whether vehicles are arranged 'side by side' or 'end to end' when they are put away for the night, and why. Let them show you on the floor, having built 'walls' around the rail shed, bus depot or airport, using bricks 'end to end'.

And pretty maids all in a row

Objectives
To develop concepts of direction and sequence.

What you need
Plastic flowers, plastic lids, Blu-Tack, shells, sand, bricks, toy cars, a cardboard box, planks, sugar paper, felt-tipped pens, pipe-cleaners, fruit and vegetables.

What to do

During floor play let the children represent outdoor objects which are seen in rows, for example, buildings, lamp-posts and fence posts. An ever-popular idea is 'Mary, Mary, quite contrary's' garden. Stick plastic flowers on to lids with Blu-Tack, or place shells in damp sand. Encourage the children to work from left to right.

Similarly, let the children mark out on a large piece of paper the spaces for cars in a car park, 'side by side'. Put the paper on top of an upturned cardboard box with a plank imitating a ramp up to the car park. A rush-hour traffic jam can be created with cars laid 'end to end' along the road and up the ramp. Pipe-cleaners stuck on lids with Blu-Tack make good lamp-posts.

Follow-up

Examine rows which can be found in nature such as peas in a pod, seeds in some fruits and vegetables, and teeth, then try to draw them.

Squashed in and spread out

Objective

To develop concepts of conservation.

What you need

A class photograph.

What to do

Show the children a class photograph and discuss the position of each child in the photograph, for instance, which row they are in, and which position along the row. Count the number of children in each row, and ask the children to stand as they were in the photograph. Let them 'squash in' and 'spread out' a number of times, each time reminding them that there are always the same number in each row.

Follow-up

Ask the children to hold up the fingers of one hand 'spread out', and tell you how many there are. Ask them to close their fingers together and tell you how many there are now. Do this repeatedly, and with toes too, as the children discover that the answer is always the same.

Row upon row

Objective

To develop pencil control.

What you need

Thick knitting needles, paper, knitting on needles, pencils or crayons, sticky tape.

What to do

Show the children some knitting, and how it is build up in rows. Using sticky tape, secure a thick knitting needle to the bottom of a piece of paper and let the children draw in the pattern of the knitting rows until they reach the top of the paper, using curvy lines and zigzags.

London Bridge

London Bridge is falling down,
Falling down, falling down.
London Bridge is falling down,
My fair lady.

Build it up with wood and clay,
Wood and clay, wood and clay.
Build it up with wood and clay,
My fair lady.

Wood and clay will wash away,
Wash away, wash away.
Wood and clay will wash away,
My fair lady.

Build it up with bricks and mortar
[etc]

Traditional

From covering space with separate objects in a row, many children become interested in joining the objects together to form a structure. 'London Bridge' offers opportunities for co-operation, as children act out the rhyme in a procession and 'repair' the bridge using materials found in the classroom. This repair work will stimulate much scientific discussion.

Bridge it

Objective
To foster design technology skills.

What you need
A camera, plastic interlocking blocks or construction toys, books about bridges, rulers, tape measures, clipboards, an easel, pencils.

What to do
If possible, take photographs of any bridges near the nursery or school. Discuss their design with the children. Put some books about bridges near the building block area to stimulate children's interest in bridge building. Also nearby, have available rulers, tape measures, clipboards or an easel, paper and pencils, to encourage the children to draw a picture of their bridge, or even to draw a plan of it beforehand.

Chain-gangs

Objective
To develop problem-solving skills.

What you need
Large wooden or plastic bricks.

What to do
Place all the bricks in one corner of the room. Explain that when the real London Bridge was built there were no cars or trucks, only horses and carts. Explain that one very hot day all the horses were ill, so the builders very quickly had to move all the bricks themselves, but they did not want to work very much as it was so hot. Can the children think of the best way to move the bricks by all working together? (in a chain-gang).

Follow-up
Use the chain-gang idea to liven up tidy-up time, perhaps to the accompaniment of music.

Billy goats on the bridge

Objective
To stimulate fantasy.

What you need
Planks, large, strong wooden platform boxes, dressing up clothes, sheets of paper, a clipboard.

What to do
Involve the children as much as possible in planning a simple production of the 'Three billy goats gruff' for the benefit of another class. Ask the children for their ideas on what to use for a safe bridge, costumes and dialogue. As this will be simple and repetitive, write out each actor's lines on paper attached to a clipboard for use during rehearsals. Let the children devise their own sound effects for the 'trip trap' sounds.

Hind Desh

Daffodils, tulips and irises
Are all different flowers
But they are made
Into one pretty garland.

All the people of the world
Are the same
Even though our faces, clothes and words
are different,
Yet we are all the same.

Traditional, adapted by Linda Mort

Moving on from the theme of joining objects together, children can be encouraged to think about how people are joined together, in friendship and at work. This adaptation of an Indian folk song is a very simple illustration of the universal truth of unity in diversity.

A bracelet of friends

Objective
To develop feelings of self-esteem.

What you need
'Pop-it' beads, threading cubes or reels, wool, darning needles, coloured sugar paper, tissue paper, coloured gummed paper, scissors, felt-tipped pens.

What to do
Show the children that although 'pop-it' beads, threading cubes and reels look good in one colour, it is much more fun to create many different patterns using a variety of colours.

Bring in a picture of an Hawaiian garland to show how colourful they can be. Simple garlands can be made by threading crumpled tissue paper on to wool, using a large darning needle. Also, show the children how to make a paper chain bracelet from coloured gummed paper. They could then choose the names of three friends and write the names of their friends, one on each link.

Follow-up
At Christmas time, the name of each child in the class could be written on the links of a long paper chain across the room.

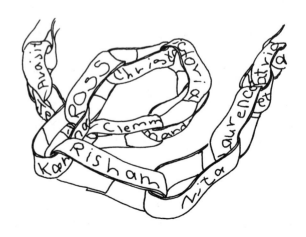

Does it matter?

Objective
To foster respect for individual differences.

What you need
No special requirements.

What to do
Use the words of the second verse of the poem to help children to relate 'parts' to the 'whole'. In this way, they will gradually come to realise that superficial differences between people are not important. Make up simple poems, such as 'Some people have green eyes, some have brown eyes and some have blue eyes, but we all have EYES!'

Follow-up
Ask the children for their views on this traditional poem:

Molly, my sister, and I fell out
And what do you think it was all about?
She loved coffee and I loved tea
And that was the reason we couldn't agree!

Sit the children in a 'sharing circle' and let each child in turn clap hands twice, and say 'My favourite drink is . . .'.

Team work

Objective
To encourage group co-operation.

What you need
Pictures of a rainbow and teams of people, for example, football teams, an alphabet and a number frieze, screw-together toys, jigsaws.

What to do
Talk about team work and show the children pictures of sports teams, air crews etc. Talk about how the dinner supervisors and the teachers work together as teams. Give each child, in a group of three, two paper segments of a rainbow and see if the 'team' can put the rainbow together on the floor. You might put one segment down to start. Similarly, give the 'teams' alphabet letters to make three-lettered words, or two numbers each to put in order up to six.

Follow-up
In twos or threes let teams co-operate in assembling screw-together toys or jigsaws.

Musical chairs

One day a boy called . . .
Came walking through the door
He picked up . . . big chairs
And put them in a very long line
All along the floor.

Then . . . began to play
A merry little tune
And . . . and . . .'s friends
Danced around the room.
[Add child's name and number of children in group].

Traditional, adapted by Linda Mort

This poem allows each individual child to be the 'star', to carry chairs (always a prestigious task) and to be the organiser of the game. As children begin to cover space with separate items, they may begin to place each item with someone/something else in mind to match with it. In this poem, the child is involved in covering the floor with a line of chairs, but also has to plan ahead as he thinks about how many chairs to put out.

I'm in charge

Objectives
To develop feelings of leadership, and one-to-one matching.

What you need
Children's chairs, a percussion instrument.

What to do
Take a group of, say, six children. One is chosen to be in charge and goes out of the room. She can only return when the rest of the group start the poem. The child must count the other children in the group and work out how many chairs are needed for a game of musical chairs. Once the child has laid out the chairs (with a reminder to carry them safely) she chooses an instrument and plays it, stopping every now and then while the rest of the children have to find an empty chair.

All aboard

Objectives
To foster oral and imaginative skills through structured play, and to develop number recognition.

What you need
Children's chairs, dressing up clothes and props (for example, for a bus conductor/

driver, air crew, space crew, naval team, train crew), sticky labels, paper, felt-tipped pens, scissors.

What to do
Ask the children if a line of chairs reminds them of anything; for instance, theatre seats or a bus, a boat, a plane, train or rocket. Let the children act out the roles of passengers, drivers, and stewards.

As a natural progression from matching to counting and number recognition, add numbered sticky labels to the seats in the theatre, boat, plane or train, and give the passengers tickets with matching numbers.

New carpet

Objectives
To develop one-to-one matching and concepts of measurement.

What you need
A home corner, carpet squares, child's dungarees, rulers, ribbon, tape measures, a clipboard, paper and pencil.

What to do
Tell the children that the home corner is to have a new carpet. Explain that the carpet will be made up from carpet squares (samples may be bought very cheaply from carpet showrooms). How can the carpet fitter work out how many squares to buy from the carpet shop? Accept all the children's ideas, and let them experiment by measuring with footsteps, using bricks, ribbon and rulers. Let the children take turns in being the carpet fitter, estimating how many carpet squares will be needed, and then laying them.

Alternative Old MacDonald

Old Macdonald had a farm
Eee-i-ee-i-o
And on that farm he had
One cow
Two horses
Three pigs
Four ducks and
Five hens.

I think you will agree with me
That Old MacDonald has a lot to see!

Linda Mort

This song/poem gives children plenty of scope to indulge their love of counting. The possibilities for adaptation are endless, for instance, 'Mrs Plum's fruit shop', 'Mr Game's Toy Shop', 'Mrs Spanner's garage' or 'Mr Turnip's allotment'. Numbers can be increased according to the children's abilities.

Down on the farm

Objective
To develop concepts of cardinal number.

What you need
Toy farm animals, hoops, sheets of paper, felt-tipped pens, transparent plastic wallets, toy vehicles.

What to do
Jot down the children's words for the song, then write them on a piece of paper near the block area. The child who is pretending to be Old MacDonald has to refer to the sheets, as he puts the right number of farm animals in each hoop on the floor.

For 'Mr Turnip's allotment', the children can draw sets of vegetables and the pictures can be slipped into transparent wallets. When selling fruit or toys, the hoops spread on the floor area give the impression of a supermarket.

For a garage, the children may need to bring toy vehicles from home (for example, one Rolls Royce, two Porsches, three Minis). In this case, make sure the owners are identified with the help of freezer labels stuck on the underside of each vehicle.

everything 1p each

Off to the supermarket

Objective
To relate concepts of cardinal number to penny shopping.

What you need
Items as for the previous idea, plus paper, a felt-tipped pen, pennies, plastic £1 coins, a purse and a shopping bag.

What to do
A toy or fruit supermarket can easily lead into a shopping activity by adding a large sign saying, 'Everything 1p each'. Use doll's house furniture to make a furniture showroom, and make a sign saying, 'Everything £1 each'. Give the children plastic £1 coins to spend.

Shopping stories

Objective
To facilitate shared reading.

What you need
Sugar paper, felt-tipped pens, staples, a large zipped bag.

What to do
Make a large shared reading book, containing the words of each child's list in a shopping song. The children will be very pleased if they are allowed to take these 'big books' home for an evening. To add to the children's sense of importance, and to protect the book, place it in a special zipped shopping-type bag, and the book should last for several weeks.

Round and round

Chapter four

Children can often be seen experimenting with circular movements such as twirling round, stirring pretend food in the home corner, running round and round, and rolling over.

The poems in this chapter have been chosen to help children investigate and develop this interest in a wide variety of ways through active learning.

Children often spontaneously spin round and round. This poem draws their attention to similar downward spiral movements in nature as the autumn leaves fall off the trees. Windy weather is sometimes rather unsettling. Discuss with the children how the word 'whirl' is evocative of the phrase 'being in a whirl', or a 'flat spin' when we have too much to do. Can the children think of a time when they are 'in a whirl', for instance, getting ready for nursery or school in the morning when everyone has overslept?

Up in the air

Objective
To develop descriptive language.

What you need
Dry autumn leaves, cardboard tubes, bottles, combs, tissue paper, nylon thread, paints, paper.

What to do
Take the children outside on a crisp autumn day and search for piles of dry leaves. Ask one child to throw some leaves in the air while everyone else has to watch very carefully as they fall. What words can they think of to describe the way they fall to the ground? (for example, spinning, whirling). Let everyone have a turn at throwing up the leaves. Now they should all stand in the middle of the pile of leaves and say the poem out loud together, everyone falling down among the leaves at the end.

After being outside, use a dance session for the children to imitate the downward spiralling of the whirling leaves. Imitate the sound of the wind by asking some children to blow down cardboard tubes, across bottle tops and, gently, on tissue paper wrapped around combs.

Follow-up
Make a hanging autumn leaves display using invisible nylon thread and either large painted leaf prints or real leaves. Attach a child's descriptive 'falling' word label to each leaf. Ensure that the leaves are hanging near a door so that they twirl in the draught.

Drop the spinner

Objective
To make children aware of both natural and manufactured spinners.

What you need
Sycamore keys, paper, card, scissors, crayons, a small battery-operated fan.

What to do
Show the children some sycamore keys and ask them how they think they will fall. Let a child stand on a chair and drop a key. What happens? After the children have played with and observed the sycamore keys for a few minutes, help them to cut out and colour their own paper spinners. Mark the children's names on the spinners before dropping them from a safe height.

Follow-up
Discuss manufactured spinners such as weather vanes and hand-held battery fans. Show the children how such a fan spins. What is the purpose of the fan? Under careful supervision, allow each child to have a turn at holding and working a fan. What can they feel on their faces?

Watch carefully

Objective
To encourage observational skills.

What you need
A smooth round pencil, coloured wool or string, sticky tape, a Helter Skelter marble game, an electric drill, a pipe-cleaner, *Creepy Castle* by John Goodall.

What to do
Wind contrasting coloured wool or string diagonally around a pencil and secure both ends with sticky tape. Let the children stand the pencil on its point and twirl it round slowly (while still holding on). What does the wool appear to be doing? Does it remind them of a fairground ride, particularly a helter skelter?

Use sections of a Helter Skelter marble run to recreate the apparent downward spiral movement of the wool or string on the pencil, and the real movement of the twirling leaves. Bring in an electric power drill and show the children the spiral form of the bits. Remind them never to touch such tools.

Follow-up
Talk through the *Creepy Castle* book and point out the spiral staircase in the castle. Let the children make a spiral staircase by winding a long thick pipe-cleaner around their finger. On removing their fingers, some children may go on to experiment with the springiness of the spiral. (See also 'Spring Time', Chapter one.)

Stirring

A stir for me,
And a stir for you,
A stir for the cat,
And the baby too.
Put in a sixpence
Just for luck.
Put in a horse-shoe
And cover it up.
Christmas is coming,
The presents are done,
Stir up the pudding
And then for the fun.

Author unknown

Children enjoy helping in the kitchen, particularly if stirring, mixing, and possibly tasting are involved. This seasonal poem could be linked with actually making a Christmas pudding at nursery or school (you could also mix a pancake for Shrove Tuesday) with the children helping to stir in the ingredients and observing the changes in the mixture. To bring the poem up to date you could substitute 'five pence' for 'sixpence'.

What shape?

Objective
To develop an awareness of the circular movement of stirring.

What you need
Duplicating paper, bowls, crayons.

What to do
Photocopy the outline of a bowl (looking from above). Give each child a crayon, telling them to imagine that the crayon is a spoon and they need to stir their mixture in the bowl on the paper. What shape is made by the crayon? Continue 'stirring' with different coloured crayons. If this activity is used as writing practice, ensure that the child stirs in an anticlockwise direction.

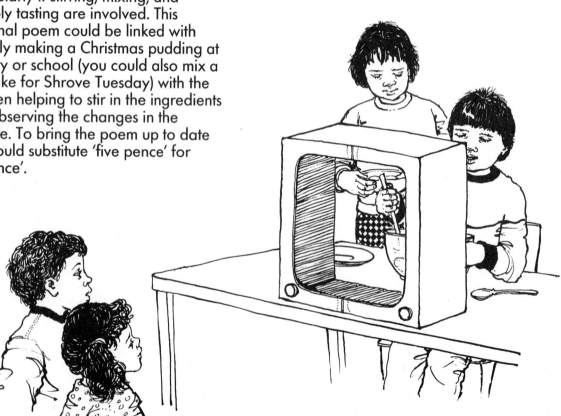

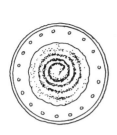   

Look what happens!

Objective
To explore the effects of mixing substances.

What you need
Powdered milk shake or milk pudding mixes, a cardboard box.

What to do
As a special treat, let the children mix powdered milk shake into their milk. Ask them what has happened to the powder as the milk shake changes colour and the powder apparently disappears.

Alternatively, make an instant milk dessert that thickens after it has been left to stand. Ask the children if they notice any difference in the mixture after a few minutes. The children will enjoy stirring the thickened mixture as they will see the patterns created by their stirring.

Follow-up
Using a cardboard box, cut out the shape of a television set and draw on dials for volume control, channels etc. After having followed a simple stirring recipe with the teacher in a small group, let the children take turns to be a television cookery expert, demonstrating how to make their favourite food. They must try to give instructions in the correct order while pretending to follow the recipe.

Mixing machines

Objective
To develop an awareness of mechanical stirrers.

What you need
Catalogue or magazine pictures, paper, a stapler, adhesive, a felt-tipped pen, a sand pit, a cardboard box, a small plastic bucket.

What to do
Stirring by hand can become very tiring after a while. Can the children think of any machines that perform the same action? Give them a clue by suggesting they think about machines used in a kitchen, such as a food processor and a hand blender, or machines used on a building site, such as a cement mixer.

Collect pictures to make a class book of mechanical stirrers, asking the children to suggest where they might be found and what they are used for.

Follow-up
Turn the sand pit into a building site and make a cement mixer with a cardboard box. Cut a round hole in one side and slot a bucket through it. The hole should be slightly larger than the bucket, allowing the bucket to be moved round by hand. Experiment with mixing mud, sand and water.

The wheels on the bus

**The wheels on the bus go round and round,
Round and round, round and round.
The wheels on the bus go round and round
All day long.**

Traditional

This rhyme has a catchy tune which is easy to remember and simple to mime. The bus can be changed to a different vehicle, for instance a lorry or milk-float, and the children can make up their own words to describe the actions of the driver, passengers or moving parts on their chosen vehicle.

Tyre fun

Objective
To develop visual and tactile discrimination.

What you need
Different sized wheels from a variety of real and toy vehicles, thick wax crayons, paper, sand, a blindfold, pictures of vehicles.

What to do
Make a display of wheels which vary in thickness, size and tyre pattern. Display pictures of different vehicles on the classroom walls. Can the children match the wheels to the vehicles? Take a wheel with a very distinctive tyre tread and ask a blindfolded child to feel the wheel and describe the pattern.

Make prints of unusual patterns by rolling the tyres in damp sand. Can the children match the patterns to the correct tyres? Start with just two or three patterns. Alternatively, show the children how to make tyre rubbings using thick wax crayons and thin sheets of paper.

Make a car

Objective
To develop design technology skills.

What you need
A toy car, cardboard boxes, dowelling, cotton reels, Plasticine.

What to do
Obtain a simply-made, hollow toy car without a bottom plate. Examine the wheels to see how they are attached in pairs by an 'axle'; probably a thin metal rod.

Take a small group of children to the craft area and help them plan what they would need to make a vehicle with moving wheels, for example, a cardboard box for the body, cotton reels for wheels, small pieces of dowelling for the axles, and a blob of Plasticine on the end of the dowelling to hold the wheels in place.

Wheely pictures

Objective
To become aware of objects which revolve.

What you need
Split pins, paper, felt-tipped pens, crayons, a stapler, scissors.

What to do
Children enjoy looking at books which involve their active participation. Link this interest with the theme of the poem by helping them to make a class book of items which revolve. Use split pins to attach the objects to a background scene so that the children can actually turn a handle, wheel or knob. Examples might include a steering wheel attached to the picture of a dashboard, or a door knob attached to a background door.

Alternatively, you could make a display of movable objects on the classroom wall. Keep them at the children's height so that they are easily accessible.

Help me wind my ball of wool

Help me wind my ball of wool,
Hold it gently, do not pull.
Wind the wool and wind the wool,
Around, around, around.

Author unknown

Children enjoy helping adults do grown-up jobs, especially if it involves changing the shape or appearance of a material (see also Chapter six). With the help of the poem, they will be fascinated by the idea of the ball of wool being a length of wool at first which is gradually built up into a big, soft ball as the wool is wound round and round. If the children can do this with very thick wool, the transformation will be even more dramatic.

Find the treasure

Objective
To develop the concept of conservation.

What you need
Pieces of thick and thin wool, a precious item, a yo-yo, a scarf.

What to do
Tie a precious object, such as a bracelet, to the end of a large ball of wool and unravel the wool around the room leaving a trail. The children must take turns in winding up the wool to find the treasure. Do the children realise that the amount of wool stays the same whether it is stretched out in a trail or wound up in a ball?

Let them compare equal lengths of thick and thin wool. Do they wind up to the same sized balls of wool?

Follow-up
Encourage the children to practise winding up other objects such as yo-yos and scarves. Sing 'Wind the bobbin up':

Wind the bobbin up,
Wind the bobbin up,
Pull, pull, clap, clap, clap;
Point to the ceiling,
Point to the door,
Point to the window,
Point to the floor.
Clap your hands together,
One, two, three,
Put your hands upon your knee.

(Traditional)

Where does it come from?

Objective
To learn about the origins of wool.

What you need
Access to a sheep farm, small pieces of sheep's wool, a volunteer knitter and spinner, an old hand-knitted jumper.

What to do
Sing 'Baa Baa Black Sheep' with the children and discuss where wool comes from. Visit a farm and, with the farmer's permission, allow the children to stroke a sheep, feeling the texture of its wool.

Try and find out how much sheep's wool is needed to knit one jumper. If possible, invite a spinner into nursery or school to demonstrate the art of spinning using a real spinning wheel. Contacts can often be made by visiting craft fairs where this skill is being demonstrated.

During another week, ask a parent or grandparent who is a keen knitter to sit in the classroom for a couple of mornings and knit part of a jumper. Examine the garment at different stages so that the children can see how the rows of stitches can be gradually transformed into a jumper. Many children will never have seen a hand-knitted garment.

Follow-up
Unravel an old hand-knitted jumper, letting the children take turns to wind up the ever-increasing ball of wool.

Make a hedgehog

Objective
To use the winding movement to help develop fine motor control.

What you need
A mug, an eggcup, card, wool, scissors, scraps of felt, adhesive.

What to do
Fold the card in two, and draw round the shape of the mug, with the circle of the eggcup in the middle. Cut out both shapes to form a 'doughnut'. Tie one end of a long piece of thick wool through the hole, and ask a child to keep threading the wool round the card and through the hole. Several layers should be built up evenly. Snip through all the strands of the wool at the outer edge of the card circles. Gently separate the circles and slip a length of wool between them. Pull the wool tight and secure all the strands of wool with a knot. The card circles may now be removed, and the wool fluffed up to make a hedgehog. Felt eyes can be stuck on.

The roundabout

The music starts and we go round,
Turning to the happy sound
On buses, bikes and aeroplanes,
Animals and coloured trains.
Round and round and round we ride
With our friends, side by side –
But soon the music starts to slow;
We wave goodbye and off we go.

Jackie Wallace

Most children love going to the fair and one of the greatest attractions is the roundabout. This rhyme conjures up an image of brightly-painted vehicles and animals, and reminds the children of the slight dizziness they feel as they reluctantly climb down at the end of the ride.

Round we go

Objective
To explore the sensation of dizziness.

What you need
Chalk, hobby-horses, fairground-type music.

What to do
Draw a large circle with chalk on the floor. Ask a small group of children to get ready for a ride on the roundabout by standing astride the hobby-horses which have been placed around the circle. Start playing the music slowly and increase the speed as the children move round the circle on their horses. Gradually slow down the music and then stop. How do the children feel? Do they still feel dizzy if they change direction after half a minute?

Miniature merry-go-round

Objective
To develop creative imagination.

What you need
A 'lazy Susan' revolving dish, Duplo animals and figures, Blu-Tack.

What to do
Recreate the fun of the merry-go-round by making a miniature version out of a revolving dish. Ask the children to choose some Duplo animals and vehicles and show them how to attach the Duplo with Blu-Tack around the edge of the dish. The children can decide where to sit the figures and then carefully spin the dish for the ride to begin.

Find the letter

Objective
To develop initial sound and letter recognition.

What you need
A cake decorating turntable, sugar paper, plastic letters, plastic animals, Blu-Tack.

What to do
Maintain the children's interest in revolving objects by using a cake decorating turntable as an aid to initial sound and letter recognition. Place the turntable in the middle of a bright sugar-paper circle, which is 8cm larger in diameter than the turntable. Space out three plastic letters including 'c' on the outer edge of the paper circle, and sit a small plastic cat on the turntable using Blu-Tack. The children can take turns to move the turntable round like a roundabout until the cat reaches its initial sound.

Vary the plastic objects and letters until all the sounds have been covered.

Follow-up
Invite a parent into nursery or school to demonstrate the real use of a cake decorating turntable. You could perhaps raffle the finished cake for school funds.

Explore other flat spinners, both large and small. Have the children ever visited a Chinese restaurant which has partly-revolving tables? Can they suggest why this is useful to a hungry diner?

The children could collect a set of toys that spin; for example, a record on a toy record player, a plunger-type spinning top, and flat metallic or wooden colour spinner. What happens to the colours as a colour spinner whizzes round?

Here is a steamroller

Here is a steamroller, rolling and rolling,
Ever so slowly, because of its load.
Then it rolls up to the top of the hill,
Puffing and panting it has to stand still.
Then it rolls . . . all the way down!

Author unknown

This poem offers a good opportunity to develop what is, for many children, a spontaneous hand action, rolling their hands one over the other, as if winding up a bobbin. The children will enjoy miming the action of the poem as it is read out, moving their hands very slowly at first and then very quickly on the last line.

You could consider taking the children to some road works to see a steamroller in action or look at other machinery which uses rollers, for example, an old-fashioned mangle or a roller for flattening grass tennis courts.

sticky tape, pencils or balls. Encourage their natural curiosity by asking them to try to push a plastic barrel or equivalent type of roller up a ramp or small hill. How does it feel? How much effort do they have to put into their pushing? How quickly does the barrel go down the slope? Do the children need to help it move downwards? Attach a doll or teddy to the inside of the barrel to give it a ride.

If you have no access to a gentle hill, try constructing a safe, wide ramp for the children to pedal up and free-wheel down on tricycles.

Children often roll themselves down slopes, enjoying the momentum and speed. Challenge them to try to roll themselves up a gentle slope – this is much harder! Act out the 'Jack and Jill'

Over it goes!

Objective
To develop an awareness of the concept of forces.

What you need
A plastic barrel, wide planks of wood or a natural slope, tricycles, a doll or teddy, string.

What to do
Young children love rolling objects along a surface; objects such as toy cars, rolls of

nursery rhyme with Jack rolling down the hill and Jill rolling after him.

Ask the children to look at the traffic on the way home. Heavy lorries and buses often move quite slowly up hilly roads and the children may not be aware of this.

Follow-up
Sing 'Ten in the bed' and act out the song with ten children lying under a king-size sheet, taking turns to roll out of the 'bed'.

With the children's help, make sausage rolls using puff pastry. Can the children make a human sausage roll by unzipping and opening out a sleeping bag and then rolling up a child inside the bag?

Roll it out

Objective
To explore the concept of conservation.

What you need
Ingredients to make jam tarts, pastry cutters, bun trays, rolling pins, aprons, access to an oven, paints, paint rollers and trays, paper, cut-out shapes, a decorator's paint roller.

What to do
Let the children, wearing aprons, use small rolling pins to roll out the pastry for jam tarts. They will realise that the harder they push down with the rolling pin, the thinner the pastry becomes, while at the same time it covers a larger area. Point out to the children that they still have the same amount of pastry, even though it is a different shape when rolled out. They will understand this better if the baking activity is followed by a lot of imaginative play with modelling dough and rolling pins. (See also 'Make a pie' in Chapter five.)

Follow-up
Let the children use hand rollers rolled in paint trays to cover sheets of paper on which cut-out shapes have been temporarily stuck down. The children can be fully involved in this activity by cutting or tearing their own paper shapes from old magazines. After rolling on the paint, remove the paper shapes to reveal white silhouettes underneath.

Borrow a full-size paint roller to show the children what a decorator sometimes uses. Can they see any advantage in using a paint roller in preference to a brush?

Coil pictures

Objective
To create three-dimensional collage using paper coils.

What you need
Brightly coloured paper, card, adhesive, scissors, sticky tape.

What to do
Cut the paper into long, narrow strips and show the children how to roll these up. Secure the ends with sticky tape and show the children how to pull or push up the centre of the coil to create a tower. Make several towers in different colours, with two cuts at the bottom of each tower to form a base. The children can cover a piece of card with adhesive and then stick on the towers to create an abstract picture. Discuss with the children what it reminds them of, perhaps a moonscape or a city centre.

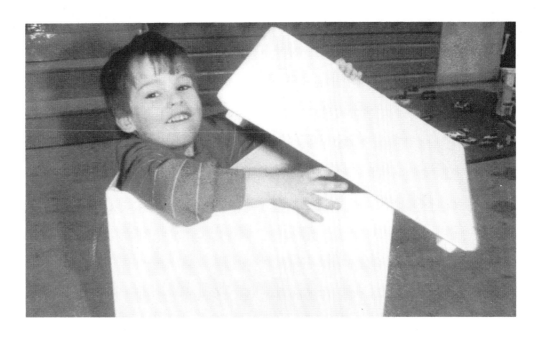

In you go

Chapter five

The idea of objects being inside something else can hold young children's interest and imagination for long periods of time. The first three songs and poems in this chapter will help children to explore the idea of surrounding or enclosing sets of items in special places, for instance zoo and farm animals.

Once children understand the notion of place, they can be helped to appreciate where a particular place is in relation to others. The poem 'In a dark, dark wood', for example, acknowledges children's fascination with the idea of a 'place within a place'.

The chapter also includes the ever-popular ring games which help to develop co-operation and trust in others. The last three songs and poems deal with a powerful idea for young children which is related to enclosure. It is the idea of something being enveloped or totally covered up, whether in a hole or a tunnel, underneath a blanket, or underneath and inside something such as a pie.

My gran's flat

My gran's flat is cosy and warm.
Four rooms to live in and a hall,
A bedroom, a bathroom, a kitchen too,
And the living room has lots for me to do.

Linda Mort

After they have heard this poem, the children can talk about the differences between houses, flats and bungalows. Why are flats so called? Talk with the children about the special sorts of activities they do at grandparents' or other relatives' or friends' homes. Are they different from their usual activities at their own home?

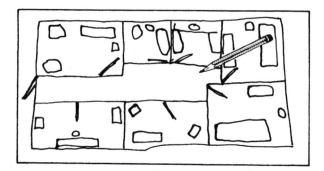

Which room?

Objective
To develop concepts of the set.

What you need
Bricks, doll's house furniture, scrap materials.

What to do
See if the children can construct an aerial view of a flat, bungalow, or the ground and first floors of a house, using play bricks to separate the rooms. Ask how they will represent a door. The children can then put the appropriate doll's furniture in each room.

Some children may like to draw a plan of their building afterwards, or even before they build it.

Follow-up
Children could build a houseboat or caravan from scrap materials.

Town and country planners

Objective
To think about how space is used.

What you need
Farm or zoo animals, model buildings, play people, miniature fencing, vehicles, sugar paper, felt-tipped pens, *A House is a House for Me* by Mary Ann Hoberman.

What to do
Talk with the children about what they can find in their favourite park, for instance areas such as pets' corner, the playground, a flower garden and a dogs' exercise ground. Let the children draw out the different areas of their park on sugar paper and place miniature buildings, people and animals on them, using fencing to separate the areas.

Follow-up
Children can make similar plans of farms, zoos, airports and sports' centres which will enable them to enclose different areas. Read *A House is a House for Me*.

Frame it

Objective
To develop concepts of spatial awareness through drawing round objects.

What you need
Bricks, sugar paper, felt-tipped pens, transparent covering film.

What to do
As children construct the outlines of buildings with bricks, they will be discussing such spatial attributes as long, short, wide, narrow, thick and thin. Reinforce this by drawing around different-shaped bricks placed on sugar paper and then covering the shapes with transparent film. The papers should be placed on shelves in the classroom so that, at tidy-up time, the children have to match the bricks to the outlines, so filling this time with a learning activity.

Follow-up
Show the children a set of Russian nesting dolls, various graded puzzles and nesting blocks, and sets of pans. The children can draw around a shape or an object, remove it and then repeat the exercise again and again until they reach the edge of the paper.

In a dark, dark wood

In a dark, dark wood there was a dark, dark house.
And in that dark, dark house there was a dark, dark room.
And in that dark, dark room there was a dark, dark cupboard.
And in that dark, dark cupboard there was a dark, dark shelf.
And on that dark, dark shelf there was a dark, dark box.
And in that dark, dark box there was a MOUSE!

Traditional

This rhyme is ideal for developing the imagination of very young children and helping to create a feeling of suspense and drama. The form of the rhyme, with its repetition and creation of excitement, appeals directly to children's sense of anticipation.

Reading the rhyme may help to reassure children who have a fear of the dark, a feeling which is experienced by almost all children at some time, to a greater or lesser degree.

The structure of the verse will appeal to those children who are fascinated by the idea of being inside something else. This concept of enclosure helps children to appreciate their own place in the world. Furthermore, the rhyme opens up children's minds to the excitement of darkness and night-time – a secret adventure in a dark place.

Night-time

Objective
To encourage language development.

What you need
A copy of *A Book of Ghosts* by Pam Adams and Ceri Jones, a doll's house with furniture, a baby doll.

What to do
Discuss with the children what it is like to see the shapes of objects in the dark. Encourage the children to describe any night frights they experienced when they were younger. Introduce *A Book of Ghosts*, which shows how ingenious cut-out shapes (such as a 'ghost') can appear scary in the dark, but are really familiar objects (such as a dressing gown) in the daylight.

Hide a baby doll in a doll's house (for example, in a pram) and ask a child to find it and point to it. When she has done so, ask, 'Where is the baby?' When the child has replied 'In the pram', ask another child, 'Where is that?'. When he replies 'In the bedroom', ask another child, 'Where is that?'. Continue with the game, including the house, the street, the town, and, if the children can understand, the country.

Hunt the mouse

Objective
To develop structured play.

What you need
A blanket, a toy mouse, a box, a torch, a home corner.

What to do
Throw a blanket over the home corner to make it dark. Let one child hide a toy mouse, preferably on a shelf in a cupboard. Ask another child to use a torch to search it out. Let a small group of children watch and recite the rhyme while the child explores the house.

Follow-up
This activity leads directly on to games of 'Hunt the thimble', in which the audience prompts the searcher by shouting 'getting warmer' or 'getting colder'.

Build a house

Objective
To develop block play.

What you need
Building blocks, a box, a toy mouse.

What to do
Encourage the children to stand large blocks vertically to represent a wood. Bricks placed flat on the floor can represent the walls of a house, with

partitioned areas inside to represent rooms. Ask the children to build a cupboard inside one room using small bricks and place a box containing a toy mouse inside the cupboard.

Follow-up
Encourage parents to play personalised versions of this rhyme at home. For example, 'In Leyton Drive there was a garden, and in this garden there was a house, and in this house there was a bedroom, and in the bedroom there was a bed, and in this bed there was a pair of pyjamas, and in this pair of pyjamas there was a boy called DARREN!'.

Dancer in the ring

There's a dancer in the ring
Tra-la-la-la-la.
There's a dancer in the ring
Tra-la-la-la-la.
There's a dancer in the ring
Tra-la-la-la-la.
For she likes sugar and I like plum.
Then you show me your motion
Tra-la-la-la-la.
Then you show me your motion
Tra-la-la-la-la.
Then you show me your motion,
For he likes sugar and I like plum.

Traditional

This lively Caribbean song, slightly adapted from the original, gives dancers an opportunity to be the centre of attraction and to improvise their own movements for others to copy. Ring games, in which one child is encircled by others, provide an enjoyable means of developing group participation and social skills. Talk to the children about the meaning of the word 'motion'.

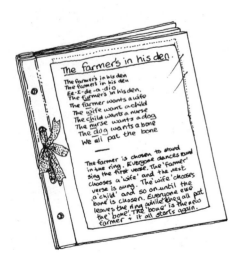

Ring games of old

Objective
To appreciate a sense of the past.

What you need
A duplicated letter to send home, clear plastic wallets, ribbon.

What to do
Send a letter home asking parents, grandparents, relatives and friends to jot down a short description of any ring games they played as a child. Alternatively, they may come and tell you, and some may be able to teach them to the children. When you have assembled several games, ideally including some from other countries, write down the instructions on cards, and place them in clear plastic wallets, tied together with ribbon. Reception children may like to show parents some of these games at an assembly.

Moving toys

Objective
To encourage language development.

What you need
A 'lazy Susan' revolving dish or a revolving cake stand, play people, Blu-Tack.

What to do
Give a child a collection of play people and ask her to stick all but one of them around the edge of a 'lazy Susan', using Blu-Tack. The remaining play figure should be placed in the centre of the dish. The child can then sing a favourite ring game, moving the play people accordingly. Children soon become engrossed in this type of activity. It is particularly beneficial for shy children as they are able to act out roles while they control the storyline.

Sing and read

Objective
To foster shared reading.

What you need
Paper, clear plastic wallets, ribbon, a cassette recorder.

What to do
Record the children singing the words of their favourite ring games, for example, 'Ring-a-ring-a-roses', 'The farmer's in his den' and the 'Hokey Cokey'. Write out the words of each song on a separate piece of paper and put them in clear plastic wallets. Tie them together with ribbon. Each child could then take home the cassette and the words to the rhymes.

A tiny, tiny worm

A tiny, tiny worm
Wriggled along the ground.
It wriggled along like this
Without a sound.

It came to a tiny hole,
a tiny hole in the ground,
It wriggled right inside,
Without a sound.

Mrs Wyn Daniel Evans

Children are usually fascinated by mini-beasts and will often sit absorbed for long periods of time observing their movements. This simple rhyme gives the children an opportunity to imitate the worm's journey with their fingers. It will also appeal to their love of 'hidey holes'.

Making a wormery

Objective
To observe worm holes and tunnels.

What you need
A tall plastic sweet jar, sand, soil, dark paper, worms.

What to do
Create a wormery in a tall plastic jar using layers of soil and sand. Help the children to collect some worms carefully from the garden and put them in the jar. Cover the sides of the jar with dark paper for about a week. This will simulate the natural conditions under the ground. Before removing the paper ask the children what changes might have occurred. When you show the children how the contents of the jar have changed, you can talk about all the worm holes and tunnels.

Match the worms

Objective
To reinforce the concept of one-to-one matching.

What you need
A shoe box and lid, coloured pipe-cleaners, felt-tipped pens, card, wool, nylon thread.

What to do
Use the idea of worms going into their holes to reinforce the concept of one-to-one matching. Pretend that coloured pipe-cleaners are worms and make worm holes in a shoe box lid. Using felt-tipped pens, make coloured rims around the holes to match the pipe-cleaners. Can the children make the worms go into their holes? Is there a hole for each worm?

Follow-up
Create a novelty greetings card using thin card and wool, so that when the card is opened a worm goes into its hole. This is done by folding a piece of card and making a hole through both layers with a hole punch. Thread the wool through from the front to the back of the card so that the wool worm hangs down at the front, and tie a knot at the back. Colour the rim of the hole brown for soil and add grass and flowers to create a garden picture. The card is now ready to open.

Feel your way

Objective
To develop confidence in moving by touch.

What you need
A blindfold, a play tunnel, blankets.

What to do
Help children to realise that underground worms have no vision at all. Using a play tunnel and a couple of blankets to crawl under, make a very simple obstacle course for the children. Blindfold a small group of children, one at a time, and see if they can still get through the obstacle course.

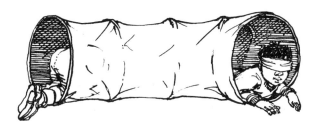

Miss Polly

Miss Polly had a dolly
Who was sick, sick, sick,
So she phoned for the doctor
To be quick, quick, quick.
The doctor came
With his bag and his hat,
And he rapped at the door
With a rat-tat-tat.

He looked at the dolly
And he shook his head.
Then he said, 'Miss Polly,
Put her straight to bed.'
He wrote on a paper
For a pill, pill, pill;
'I'll be back in the morning
With my bill, bill, bill.'

Traditional

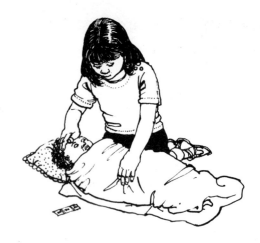

This song provides something extra to the usual game of doctors and nurses. The words are easy to remember and the actions can either be performed by just two children pretending to be Miss Polly and the doctor, or by the whole group miming all the actions, while singing the song. Although it is not mentioned in the song, the children's first instinct would probably be to cover up the doll with blankets.

Wrap the baby up warm

Objective
To explore the concept of having a high temperature.

What you need
A strip thermometer, a doll, various baby blankets.

What to do
Discuss with the children why we cover ourselves up with sheets and blankets or a duvet at night. How would mummy or daddy check whether the baby had a high temperature? Show the children a strip thermometer and demonstrate how it works on a child's forehead by changing colour as the temperature changes.

Talk about high temperatures. How do we feel when we have a high temperature? Do parents always put more blankets on the bed? Discuss how the correct procedure for high temperatures would be to try to cool down the child by removing some bedding and sponging him or her with tepid water. Help the children to grasp the idea by giving them a pretend strip thermometer and a sponge and a bowl of tepid water in the play area. These should, of course, be used under careful supervision.

Follow-up
Show the children a wall thermometer and explain how it measures the temperature of the air.

Take her out for some fresh air

Objective
To explore ways of keeping a baby warm.

What you need
A variety of baby blankets, baby-gros, mittens, snow suits, hats, a baby nest.

What to do
Discuss with the children what could be wrong with the doll in the song. If she had a bad cold, after a couple of days she could be allowed out for some fresh air. How would the children keep the doll warm if she were taken out in a pram on a frosty day?

Make a display of outdoor baby clothes such as mittens, snow suits and hats with ear flaps. Explain how important it is to keep a baby's head covered on a cold day. Look at different types of baby blankets. How do cellular blankets with holes keep a baby warm? Let the children use a baby nest in the home corner as an alternative to the usual cot.

Hello, is that the doctor's surgery?

Objective
To develop communication skills through role-playing.

What you need
Home corner furniture, a doll, a table, a telephone, a writing pad, pens/pencils, a toy medical kit.

What to do
Help the children to use the home corner to act out the story of Miss Polly. They should improvise the words, including the telephone call to the doctor's surgery. Can they describe the baby's symptoms to the doctor? Use a table in the home corner for the doctor to write out a prescription for the sick baby.

Little Jack Horner

**Little Jack Horner
Sat in a corner
Eating his Christmas pie;
He put in his thumb
And pulled out a plum,
And said,
'What a good boy am I!'**

Traditional

This traditional nursery rhyme is easy to remember, even for very young children. It appeals to children's sense of anticipation as they wonder what is under the pastry lid. While most children are unlikely to actually put their hands in a pie they do enjoy the element of chance involved in putting their hands in a lucky dip or bran tub and pulling out a prize.

Make a pie

Objective
To explore the concept of covering area.

What you need
Individual foil containers from small pies, Plasticine, rolling pins, circle shapes, scissors, *Melanie Mall and the Pie in the Sky* by Chloë Keef.

What to do
Make pretend fruit pies by rolling out Plasticine thinly. Talk about how to put the pastry in the foil containers, plus a Plasticine fruit filling and a lid.

Explore ways of cutting the Plasticine to the right size and shape, for example using a plastic circle or toy saucer as a cutter. Let the children take turns to describe the fruit filling in the pie for the others to guess.

To stimulate their imagination, read *Melanie Mall and the Pie in the Sky*.

Food surprises

Objective
To develop prediction skills.

What you need
Magazine pictures, paper to make a scrap-book, a stapler, adhesive, a toasted sandwich maker, bread, sandwich fillings.

What to do
Discuss both sweet and savoury food surprises in which one ingredient covers another. Cut out recipe pictures from magazines to make a scrap-book. Look through the pictures and tell the children what the top ingredient is and ask them to think what could be underneath. The pictures might include shepherd's pie, lasagne, trifle and fruit crumble.

Follow-up
Bring a sandwich maker into nursery or school. How many fillings can the children think of to go inside sandwiches? Experiment by making some of the toasties. Write out your favourite toastie recipe for shared reading with parents.

What flavour?

Objective
To develop the sense of taste.

What you need
A variety of individual fruit pies, spoons, a blindfold, cooking apples, access to a cooker.

What to do
Pretend that you run a bakery. One day, you were feeling very tired and jumbled up all the fruit pies. Can the children take turns to identify the fruit fillings by taste only, while wearing a blindfold? Which one do they like best?

Follow-up
Make some stewed apple with the children to use as a pie filling. Discuss the changes in texture that take place.

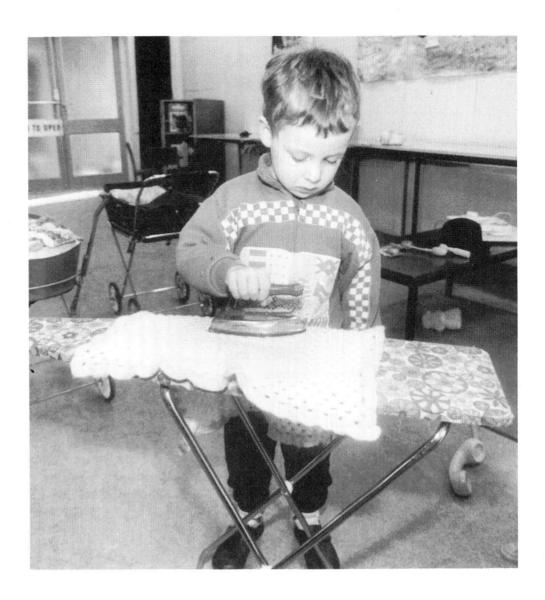

Fancy that!

Chapter six

Children have a strong interest in how things change, whether it is in the apparent magic worked by machines such as photocopiers or the sun's effect on an ice lolly. Similarly, they enjoy bringing about changes themselves, experimenting with colour, generating new ideas through creative thought, and on the emotional level, exploring mood changes.

Can you tell me

Can you tell me, can you tell me
What the typists are doing?
They are tapping, they are tapping,
So I will tap too.

Can you tell me, can you tell me,
What the window cleaners are doing?
They are wiping, they are wiping,
So I will wipe too.

Can you tell me, can you tell me,
What the tailors are doing?
They are sewing, they are sewing,
So I will sew too.

Author unknown

Children are often fascinated by the work which adults do, especially when basic materials are transformed into something new. They are usually very enthusiastic about having a go for themselves. This easy song gives an ideal opportunity for the children both to mime the actions and to examine in closer detail the type of work involved in each verse.

Press there

Objective
To explore cause and effect in relation to pressing buttons and keys.

What you need
An obliging secretary, a typewriter, a photocopier, a push-button telephone, a toy computer, a calculator and other push-button machines.

What to do
From a very young age, children enjoy pressing buttons to make things work. Give them some first-hand experience of the 'tapping' of the typist by taking a small group of children to visit the nursery or school secretary. Encourage the children to ask her about her job and, under careful supervision, let them type out a brief message on the typewriter. How do the children think the letters appear on the previously blank paper?

Examine a photocopier with the children. By pressing a square button, the children will see how one sheet of paper can 'magically' be copied several times. The children will be thrilled by having their own pictures copied to give to parents and friends.

Back in the classroom, let the children help set up a push-button office in the play area using an old telephone, calculators and toy computers and typewriters. If possible, have a real, but old, typewriter on display for the children to explore.

Cleaning up

Objective
To develop reasoning skills.

What you need
Magazine pictures of items to be cleaned, cleaning tools and materials.

What to do
Children often enjoy helping adults to clean up around the house, particularly when they can see a real change or transformation in whatever they are polishing, from dirty to sparkling clean. Encourage them to help clean the equipment at nursery or school at the end of a week or at half-term and discuss what sort of cleaning materials to use for each area of the room, for instance a brush and pan might be suitable for a sandy floor, whereas diluted washing-up liquid and cloths might be best for wiping off fingerprints from the play area furniture.

Develop the children's reasoning skills by asking them to match pictures of objects to be cleaned with the correct tool or materials to clean them; for example, a duster for ornaments and a brush for a kitchen floor.

Follow the pattern

Objective
To appreciate the transformation of two-dimensional shapes into three-dimensional shapes by sewing.

What you need
A pattern for an item of clothing, fabric, a willing parent volunteer, Polydrons, hessian, templates, needles and thread.

What to do
Although sewing cards and pictures are fairly common in nursery schools and infant classrooms, not many children will have actually seen a tailor at work. Bring some sewing skills into the nursery or school by inviting a parent to demonstrate how an item of clothing is made from scratch using a paper pattern. Can the children see any similarity between a paper pattern being laid on a piece of fabric and themselves putting a template on a piece of paper, drawing round it and cutting out the shape?

If the children can watch the pieces of fabric being sewn together on a sewing machine, they will witness the fabric being transformed from a two-dimensional to a three-dimensional shape.

This concept can be imitated by the children using a construction kit such as Polydron (see also 'The triangle song') in which a net can be put together to form a solid shape.

Follow-up
Using brightly coloured pieces of hessian and rectangular card or plastic templates, older children can follow a 'pattern' and sew a very simple pencil holder.

Thunder

I hear thunder.
I hear thunder.
Hark! Don't you?
Hark! Don't you?
Pitter-patter, raindrops,
Pitter-patter, raindrops,
I'm wet through,
So are you.

Author unknown

Many children are frightened of thunderstorms, disliking the crash of thunder and the sudden flashes of lightning. Use this rhyme, which can be sung to the tune of 'Frère Jacques', as a starting point for confronting this fear.

Sit the children in a circle and let them take turns to share their feelings about what makes them frightened in stormy weather, for instance, the noise of the wind or dustbins falling over. The children will soon realise that they are not alone in their fears.

Use percussion instruments to imitate the sound of the thunder and raindrops; a drum for the thunder and bells or a tambourine for the rain. Alternatively, encourage the children to mime the actions with their fingers.

Keeping the doll dry

Objective
To develop an awareness of waterproof materials.

What you need
Three dolls, a selection of fabric to use as cloaks (some waterproof), tape, a selection of outdoor coats.

What to do
Take three pieces of fabric (one waterproof) and cut out three cloak shapes to fit the dolls, sewing or sticking tape on the neck edges for easy attachment. Let the children dress the dolls in their usual clothes, plus one cloak each for their outer garments. Leave the dolls outside on a rainy day for about an hour. Can the children guess which doll will remain the dryest? When the time is up, the children can remove the cloaks to see who guessed correctly.

Follow-up
Compare raincoats and anoraks. Does anyone have a plastic coat? What happens to the rain as it splashes on a plastic coat?

Wet play

Objective
To develop an awareness of changes that occur when objects are placed in water.

What you need
A chamois leather, a woollen jumper, cotton wool, sponges, loofahs, a magic painting book.

What to do
Have the children ever helped a parent to wash some clothes by hand? Wash a jumper with a small group of children. Let them feel the weight of the jumper before it goes into the water and then after it has been soaked. What changes do they notice?

Take the children outside to wash a car (with permission). Handle a dry chamois leather and discuss how it feels. Then dip it in the warm soapy water. What changes in texture can be felt?

Follow-up
Experiment by dropping cotton wool, sponges and loofahs into water.

Encourage the children to describe what happens to them when they are wet. Look at 'magic' changes that can occur with water; for instance, in magic painting books where the coloured picture appears when water is brushed over the page. Try to obtain a novelty paper flower that 'blossoms' under water.

Rainbow painting

Objective
To develop an awareness of pattern.

What you need
A child's watering-can, mixed powder paint, a plastic sheet, large pieces of paper, a water trough, waterproof aprons, water droppers.

What to do
Children sometimes comment on the circular shape made by raindrops as they bounce off a car windscreen. Simulate these patterns by letting the children pour a full watering-can into a water trough. Can they see the tiny circles made by the water droplets?

Cover the floor with a large plastic sheet and place a large piece of paper on top. Ensure the children are wearing waterproof aprons and then encourage them to pour a child's paint-filled watering-can on to the paper, moving their arms backwards and forwards to make a pattern.

Clip another sheet of paper to an easel and show the children how to squeeze droplets of paint from a water dropper on to the top of the sheet; watch how they run down, just like raindrops. Experiment with different colours to make an abstract picture.

She fell into the bath-tub

She fell into the bath-tub,
She fell into the sink,
She fell into the raspberry jam
And
    came
       out
          pink.

Author unknown

This is a fun, nonsense poem that is simple and easy to learn. Children love experimenting and observing changes in their concoctions. The idea of someone falling into jam and coming out pink will also appeal to their sense of humour.

To develop skills of prediction, the poem could be acted out using Playmobile figures wearing white scraps of material. The children can guess what colour they will become when dipped in saucers of different types of jam.

Reading together

Objective
To develop pre-reading skills.

What you need
Card, a felt-tipped pen, clear sticky film.

What to do
Write out the poem on a thick piece of card, about A4 size, and cover with clear sticky film for protection. The children should, in turn, take the card home for shared reading with parents. The adult should read the poem to the child, pointing to each word, then they should both read together. The child could then attempt to read the poem on her own.

Follow-up
Make up class nonsense rhymes using different colours for the last line.

It's magic

Objective
To develop observational skills.

What you need
Flour, water, oil, salt, food colouring, a large bowl, *Teddy Bears One to Ten* by Susanna Gretz.

What to do
Make some modelling dough by mixing together the flour, water, oil, and salt. Knead it until it is soft and smooth. Let a group of children take turns in adding a few drops of food colouring to the dough. If the colouring is initially deep red, can the children predict the eventual colour of the dough? Mix the food colouring into the dough. What stages do the colours go through? Look out for a pretty marbled effect before the dough eventually turns pink.

Follow-up
Read *Teddy Bears One to Ten* in which the teddy bears are dipped in dye.

How does it look?

Objective
To develop an awareness of colour mixing.

What you need
Cardboard, scissors, blue cellophane, *Bethy Wants a Blue Ice-cream* by Bill Gillam.

What to do
Make some cardboard spectacles for the children and insert blue cellophane for the lenses. Let the children experiment with looking through the glasses. Can they predict what will happen if they look at something yellow? Read *Bethy Wants a Blue Ice-cream*, a story about a little girl who will not be satisfied until she has a blue ice-cream. The children could then act out the story of Bethy.

Follow-up
Experiment with torches that have different coloured lenses, and if possible go outside on a dark winter's afternoon to shine them on bushes and trees. Hallowe'en would be a good time to create an eerie atmosphere!

Stamping

**Stamping, stamping all about –
I am letting my feelings out;
Stamping, stamping all about –
I am letting my feelings out;
I'll stamp hard, I'll stamp strong,
Until my feelings have all gone!**

Brenda I. Piper

This poem gives the children an opportunity to vent their occasional very strong feelings of anger. Acting out the poem can provide an outlet for pent-up aggression. It can also be used as a starting point for discussing what makes the children angry – perhaps when the children are sitting in a circle.

How do the children behave when they are cross? Does this have any effect on other people, for instance their parents? By talking about emotions, even very young children can begin to recognise that they can control their own behaviour. The transformation comes in changes of emotion, from being angry to feeling more relaxed.

Make her happy

Objective
To encourage a caring attitude towards others.

What you need
A rag doll with two faces – one happy, one sad.

What to do
Hold the sad face of the rag doll to the children and ask them why they think the doll is sad and how can they cheer her up? If you think they have achieved this, show them the doll's happy face.

Can they think of examples at the nursery or school when someone has been upset and they have comforted the child and made him feel better?

What makes me angry

Objective
To develop an awareness of angry and happy feelings.

What you need
Paper, felt-tipped pen, crayons.

What to do
Fold in half enough sheets of paper for the whole class. Draw two blank faces on each sheet. Ask the children to make one face angry and one face happy. Help them to write underneath what makes them angry and what makes them happy. The children would also be interested in seeing you drawing happy and sad faces and discussing what makes you angry or happy.

Should they be angry?

Objective
To explore the feeling of anger through modern stories.

What you need
A copy of *The Paper Bag Princess* by Robert Munsch.

What to do
Read *The Paper Bag Princess* to the children and talk about why the prince and princess were cross with each other. Was the prince right to be cross with the princess for looking a mess when she had put so much effort into rescuing him? Was the princess justified in feeling cross with the prince?

Can the children think of any occasion when it is all right to show feelings of anger? (for example, if they are approached by a stranger).

The triangle song

This is a triangle,
Look and you'll see
One edge, another edge,
And a third makes three.

This is a triangle,
Look and you'll see
We can imagine all the
Things it can be.

Add a big bobble here;
Now it's a hat on a clown.
Add a broomstick and a cat;
Now it's a witch with a frown.

Draw some waves from the deep blue sea;
Now it's a sail on a boat.
Make it of metal and give it a tap;
A triangle plays a nice note.

Jane Sebba

From babyhood, children are constantly exploring shapes with their mouths, fingers and bodies. By the time they reach nursery, they are beginning to show an interest in two-dimensional shapes. This poem goes beyond simple shape discrimination and encourages the children to use their imagination — what can the triangle be transformed into?

Hunt the triangle

Objective
To develop an awareness of shape in the environment.

What you need
A duplicated letter home.

What to do
After reading this poem to the children, take them on a triangle hunt around the nursery or school. How many objects can they find that use triangles in their design? In a duplicated letter to parents, ask them to join in the search for triangles around the house.

Follow-up
Use this method for other shapes, such as squares, circles and rectangles.

What can it be?

Objectives
To develop the skills of listening, co-operation and imaginative thought.

What you need
Photocopied sheets, each containing four triangles, large sheets of paper, crayons, gummed triangles, a copy of *Shapes* by Janet Williams.

What to do
Give four children a sheet of paper each containing four triangles. Encourage them to listen carefully to each other's imaginative ideas by asking each child in turn to decide what one of the triangles could become. When a child has described her object, the whole group can attempt to draw it on their own pieces of paper. Continue until all four children have made a suggestion for the triangle and they have all been drawn.

Follow-up
Give pairs of children a large sheet of paper, crayons and a gummed paper triangle. Ask them to work together to make the triangle part of a picture — for example, a sail on a boat — and to draw in the background. The pairs can then talk about their picture to the rest of the class.

Read *Shapes* to stimulate the children's ideas.

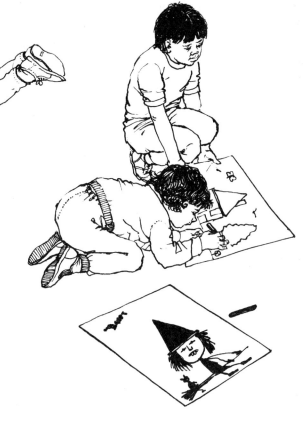

What can you make?

Objective
To develop an awareness of the relationship between two-dimensional and three-dimensional shapes.

What you need
Polydron triangles, Playmobile people.

What to do
Young children enjoy fitting shapes together. Polydron triangles give children the opportunity both to explore tessellation patterns and to construct a net that can be turned into a three-dimensional shape. Encourage the children to use the Playmobile people alongside their Polydron constructions and whole new villages will be created.

The lollipop

A lollipop who was cold
Decided to be very bold.
He went and sat out in the sun,
But all at once began to run.
He melted quickly on the floor,
And then, of course, he was no more.

Jackie Wallace

This nonsense poem introduces children to the concept of melting. Most children will have experienced trying to eat a lolly or an ice-cream on a hot day and will remember how soon it can become a sticky mess.

The rhyme can also be used as a starting point for exploring the properties of ice.

What flavour would you like?

Objective
To develop the concept of liquid freezing into ice.

What you need
Ice lolly moulds, various fruit juices, an ice-cream chart, access to a freezer.

What to do
On a summer's day, children's hearing suddenly becomes very acute to the sound of an ice-cream van and children usually have a very strong opinion about what flavour lolly they would like. Develop this interest by encouraging the children to make their own lollies from fruit juices. Let them taste the juices before they are poured into the lolly moulds, and discuss their flavours and colours. How long do the children think the lollies will take to freeze? Take them out of the freezer from time to time to have a quick look, without dislodging the lolly sticks. When they are frozen, let the children taste them. Can they notice any differences in flavour and colour? Borrow an ice-cream chart from a local shop to discuss lolly names. Can the children think up some good names for their home-made lollies?

One freezing cold night . . .

Objective
To develop imaginative story-making.

What you need
A small plastic dog, a plastic tumbler, access to a freezer, a doll's house.

What to do
Explain to the children that you are going to make up a story together about a little dog who goes for a walk on a freezing cold night. Sit them in a circle and show them the little dog, just emerging from a doll's house. Discuss where it is going and what the weather might be like in the middle of winter. Going round the circle, bounce the story from child to teacher and back to the next child, making up one sentence each. Finish with the teacher who can leave the dog lost in the dark, dripping wet, having fallen into a big barrel of water.

Put the dog into a plastic tumbler of water. Tell the children that the story will be continued later in the day and, when they are not looking, put the tumbler in the freezer. Later on, having retrieved the tumbler and reformed the circle, discuss how the poor dog has turned into a frozen block of ice. Continue with the story, having a search party out looking for the dog on the next day (which turns out to be hot). Leave the frozen block in a warm place where the children can see it melting. Finish the story with the wet, but relieved, dog finding its way home again.

Follow-up
Show the children pictures of very cold countries where it is icy all the year round. Discuss how Eskimos used to make shelters out of blocks of ice during hunting expeditions.

Frozen peas

Objective
To develop the concept of preserving by freezing.

What you need
500g fresh peas in their pods, access to a freezer, microwave or stove, a tray, a bowl.

What to do
Take a bag of fresh peas into nursery or school and let the children shell them into a bowl. Spread them out on a tray and freeze them. Encourage the children to examine them again. What differences do they find? What do they feel like?

If possible, defrost some peas in a microwave, and leave others to thaw at room temperature. Which is quicker? How does this help a parent hurrying to cook an evening meal?

Cook the peas either in the microwave or on a stove. What changes in texture do the children notice now?

Leave a few pea pods out in the classroom. What happens to them after a few days? Why are some foods kept in a freezer?

Book list

Extending Thought in Young Children – A parent-teacher partnership,
Chris Athey (Paul Chapman).
Tom's Cat, Charlotte Voake (Walker Books).
Up and Up, Shirley Hughes (Bodley Head).
Come Away from the Water, Shirley, John Burningham (Jonathan Cape).
Meg at Sea, Helen Nicholl and Jan Pienkowski (Puffin).
Bears in the Night, Stan and Jan Berenstain (Collins).
Fifteen Ways to Go to Bed, Kathy Henderson (Macdonald).
Where's Spot? Eric Hill (Puffin).
Creepy Castle, John Strickland Goodall (Macmillan).
A House is a House for Me, Mary Ann Hoberman (Viking Press).
A Book of Ghosts, Pam Adams and Ceri Jones (Child's Play).
Melanie Mall and the Pie in the Sky, Chloë Keef (Frederick Warne).
Teddy Bears One to Ten, Susanna Gretz (Collins).
Bethy Wants a Blue Ice-cream, Bill Gillham (Methuen).
The Paper Bag Princess, Robert Munsch (Hippo).
Shapes, Janet Williams (Ernest Benn).

Other Scholastic books

Bright Ideas

The *Bright Ideas* books provide a wealth of resources for busy primary school teachers. There are now more than 20 titles published, providing clearly explained and illustrated ideas on topics ranging from *Word Games* and *Science* to *Display* and *Classroom Management*. Each book contains material which can be photocopied for use in the classroom.

Teacher Handbooks

The *Teacher Handbooks* give an overview of the latest research in primary education, and show how it can be put into practice in the classroom. Covering all the core areas of the curriculum, the *Teacher Handbooks* are indispensable to the new teacher as a source of information and useful to the experienced teacher as a quick reference guide.

Management Books

The *Management Books* are designed to help teachers to organise their time, classroom and teaching more efficiently. The books deal with topical issues, such as *Parents and Schools* and organising and planning *Project Teaching*, and are written by authors with lots of practical advice and experiences to share.

Let's Investigate

Let's Investigate is an exciting range of photocopiable activity books giving open-ended investigative tasks. Designed to cover the 6 to 12-year-old age range these books are ideal for small group or individual work. Each book presents progressively more difficult concepts and many of the activities can be adopted for use throughout the primary school. Detailed teacher's notes outlining the objectives of each photocopiable sheet and suggesting follow-up activities have been included.